Handwriting Without Tears®
by Learning Without Tears

Name:

Try the new Digital Student App! Students can complete assignments, access letter formation tools, and work from home or school.

hwt-student.lwtears.com

My Printing Book

logs   truck   tunnel

LEARNING
Without Tears®

8001 MacArthur Blvd
Cabin John, MD 20818
LWTears.com | 888.983.8409

Author: Jan Z. Olsen, OTR
Content Advisors: Christina Bretz, MS, OTR/L, Tania Ferrandino, OTR/L
Illustrators: Jan Z. Olsen, OTR, Julie Koborg
Graphic Designers: Carol Johnston, Julie Koborg
Editors: Annie Cassidy, Kathryn Fox

Copyright © 2022 Learning Without Tears
Twelfth Edition
ISBN: 978-1-952970-77-1
123456789RPR242322
Printed in the USA

The contents of this consumable workbook are protected by US copyright law. If a workbook has been purchased for a child, the author and Learning Without Tears give limited permission to copy pages for additional practice or homework for that child. No copied pages from this book can be given to another person without written permission from Learning Without Tears.

Dear Student,

This book has letters, words, and sentences. You can color the pictures, too.

Sincerely,
Jan Z. Olsen

Aa	Bb	Cc	Dd	Ee	Ff	Gg	Hh	Ii	Jj	Kk	Ll	Mm
22	58	14	24	34	60	26	56	32	44	40	38	54

TABLE OF CONTENTS

Getting Started
Letter to Students 1
Table of Contents 2–3
Paper Placement & Pencil Skills 4
Learn & Check 5
Capitals, Lowercase Letters & Numbers 6
Help Me Write My Name 7

Capitals
Frog Jump Capitals
F E D P B R N M 8–9

Starting Corner Capitals
H K L U V W X Y Z 10

Center Starting Capitals
C O Q G S A I T J ... 11
Capital Review 12
Number Review 13

Teach numbers with capitals.
See teaching guidelines in the teacher's guide.

Lowercase Letters
Same as Capitals and t
c + o 14–15
s + activity 16–17
v + w 18–19
t + words 20–21

Magic c Letters
a + words 22–23
d + sentences 24–25
g + words 26–27
    activities 28–29

More Vowels
u + words 30–31
i + sentences 32–33
e + words 34–35
    activities 36–37

Transition Group
l + sentences 38–39
k + words 40–41
y + sentences 42–43
j + words 44–45
    activities 46–47

Nn	Oo	Pp	Qq	Rr	Ss	Tt	Uu	Vv	Ww	Xx	Yy	Zz
52	15	48	62	50	16	20	30	18	19	64	42	66

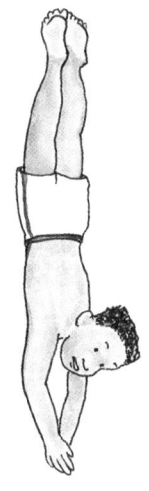

Diver Letters
p + sentences 48–49
r + words 50–51
n + sentences 52–53
m + words 54–55
h + sentences 56–57
b + words 58–59

Final Group
f + sentences 60–61
q + words 62–63
x + sentences 64–65
z + words 66–67

Numbers

Numbers on the Slate Chalkboard 88
1, 2, 3, 4, 5, 6 89–91
7, 8 92
9, 10 93

Final Check 94

Writing Activities
Writing - Plurals - Add s 17
Writing - Magic c Letters 28
The Hand Activity 29
Rhymes 36
Punctuation - Ending 37
Words - Magic c Silly Spelling Words 46
Writing - Line Practice 47
Words - Compound Words 68
Poem - "Teeth" 69
Sentences - Tunnels 70
Paragraph - Dams 71
Chant - Potatoes 72
Poem - "Counting Toes" 73
Paragraph - Bones 74
Paragraph - Shells 75
Vowels - a, e, i, o, u + y 76
Poem - "Looking for Carrots" 77
Question & Answer - Bike/Car 78
Paragraph - Truck 79
Abbreviations - Calendar 80
Capitals - Usage 81
Words - Homophones 82
Writing - Money 83
Syllables - cat-er-pil-lar 84
Paragraph - Insects 85
Sentences - Prepositions 86
Sentences - Order 87

Paper Placement & Pencil Skills

LEFT-HANDED
Place the **left** corner higher.

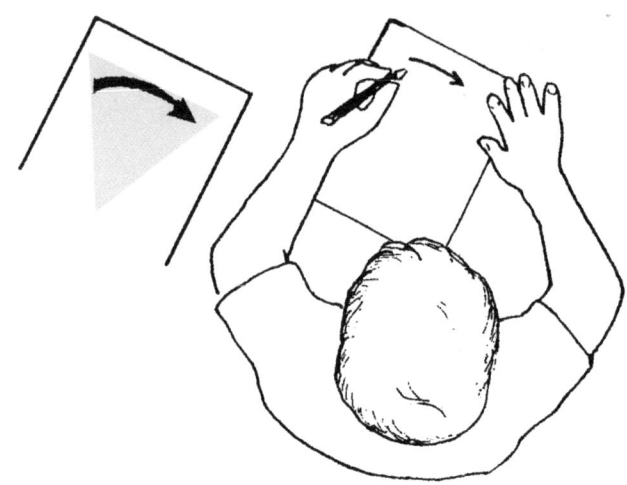

RIGHT-HANDED
Place the **right** corner higher.

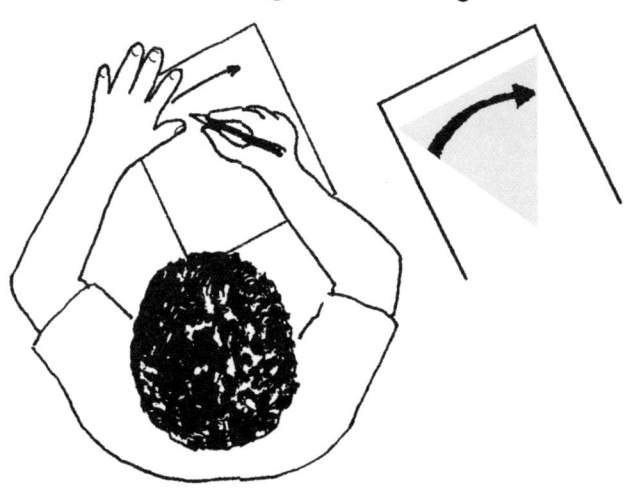

Eraser points to **left** shoulder.

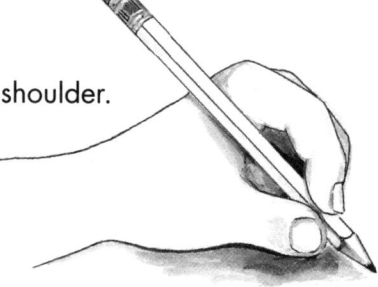

Standard grip: Hold pencil with **thumb + index finger.** Pencil rests on middle finger.

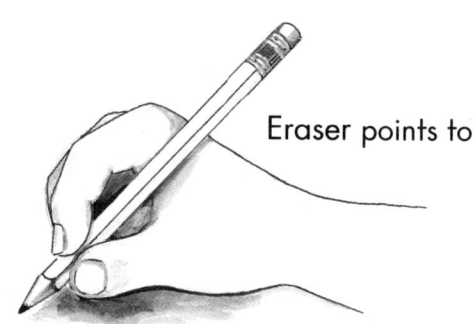

Eraser points to **right** shoulder.

Alternate grip: Hold pencil with **thumb + index and middle fingers.** Pencil rests on ring finger.

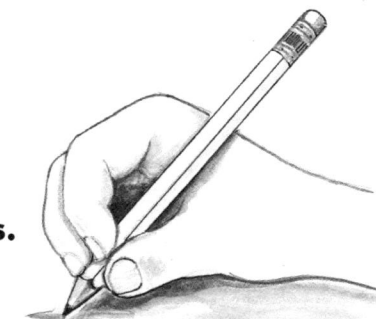

Learn & Check

Learn letters, words, sentences, and how to check them.
When you see the box , it's time to check your work.

✓ Check letter
Teachers: Help children ✓ their letter for correct start, steps, and bump.

1. Start correctly.
2. Do each step.
3. Bump the lines.

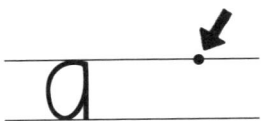  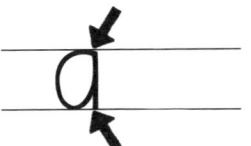

✓ Check word
Teachers: Help children ✓ their word for correct letter size, placement, and closeness.

1. Make letters the correct size.
2. Place letters correctly: tall, small, or descending.
3. Put letters close.

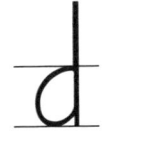  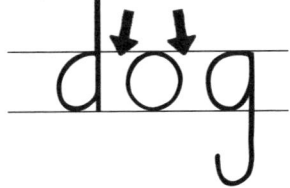

Tall   **Small**   **Descending**

✓ Check sentence
Teachers: Help children ✓ their sentence for correct capitalization, word spacing, and ending punctuation.

1. Start with a capital.
2. Put space between words.
3. End with **.** **?** or **!**

Capitals, Lowercase Letters & Numbers

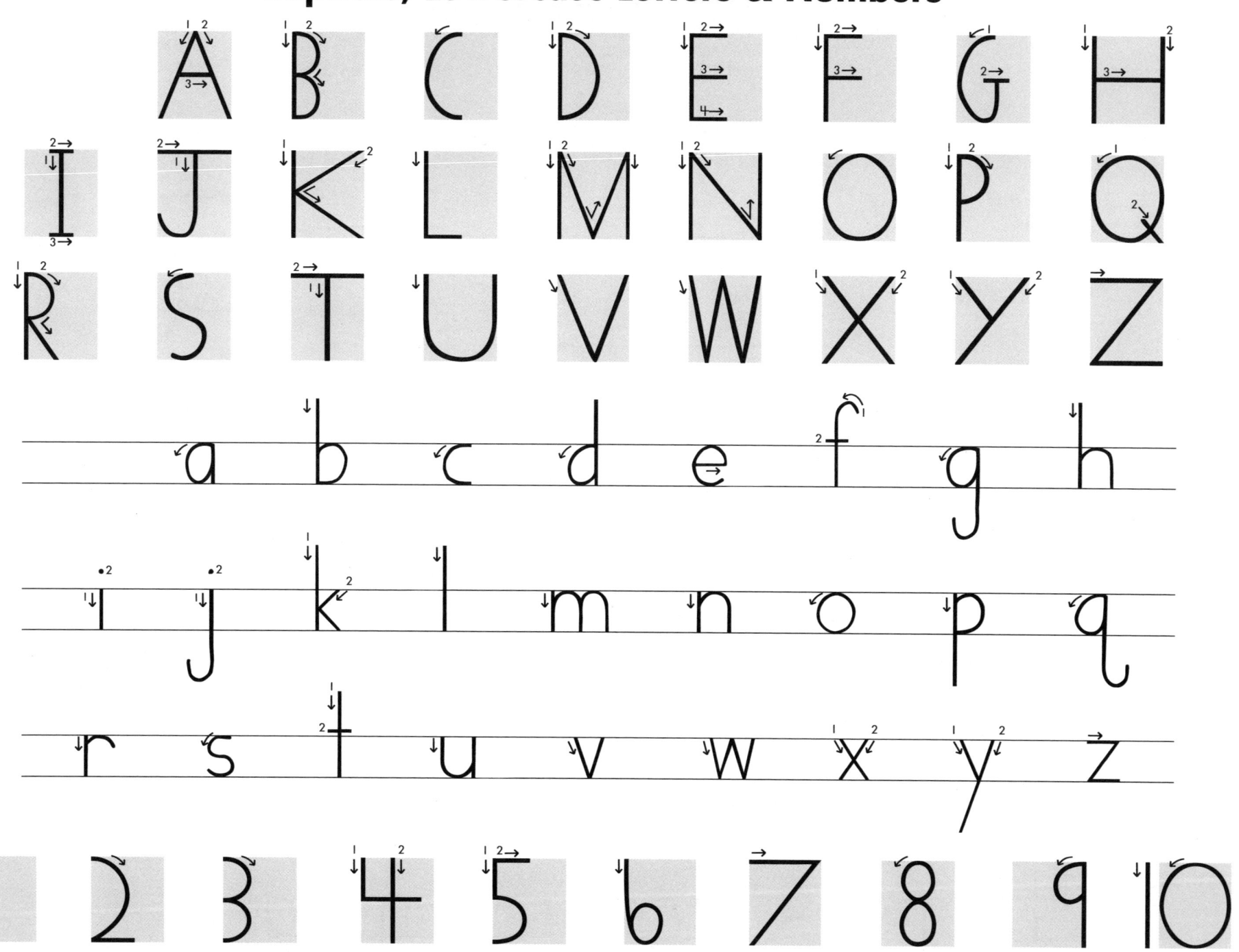

Help Me Write My Name

Add teeth. WWW MMM

Add wool. ⓒ

Teacher demonstrates.
Child copies below.

Name:

Add grass. |¹|

FROG JUMP CAPITALS

F E D P B R N M are the Frog Jump Capitals.

Frog Jump Capitals start in the Starting Corner on the dot.
Make a Big Line down.
Frog Jump back to the Starting Corner.
Now you are ready to finish the letter.

FROG JUMP CAPITALS

Start in the Starting Corner. Make a Big Line down. Frog Jump back to the Starting Corner. Finish the letter.

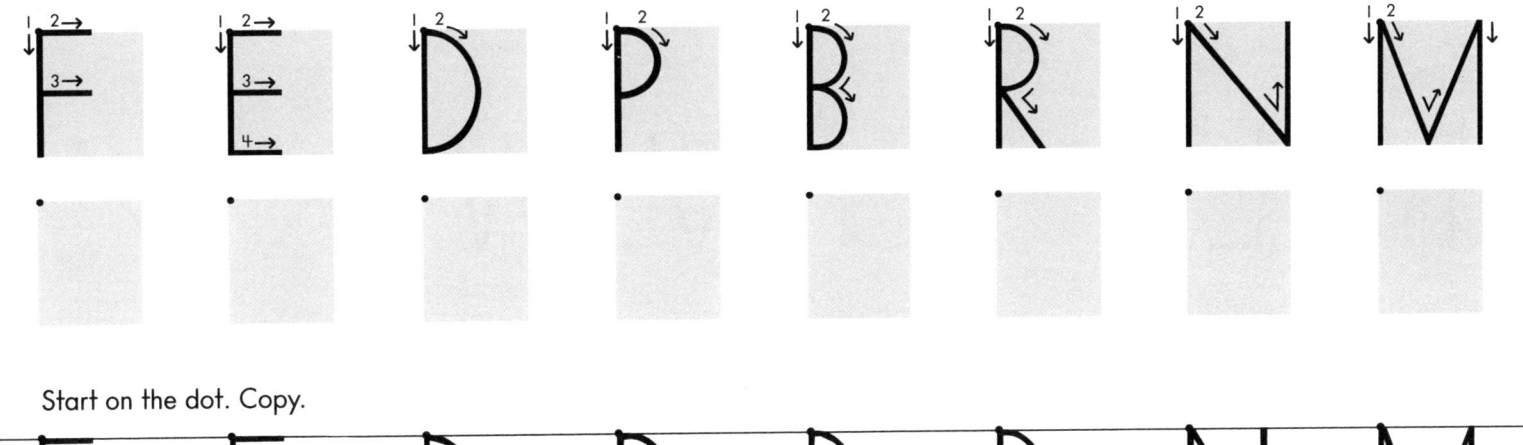

Start on the dot. Copy.

MYSTERY LETTER GAME FOR FROG JUMP CAPITALS

Start in the Starting Corner. Make a Big Line down. Frog Jump back to the Starting Corner.
Wait for your teacher to tell you which Frog Jump Capital to make.

© 2022 Learning Without Tears   *My Printing Book*

STARTING CORNER CAPITALS

H K L U V W X Y Z are Starting Corner Capitals.

Start in the Starting Corner. Copy.

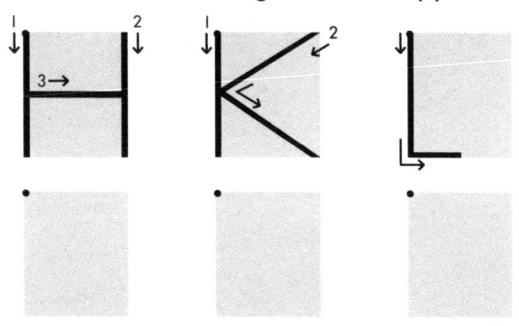

Start on the dot. Copy.

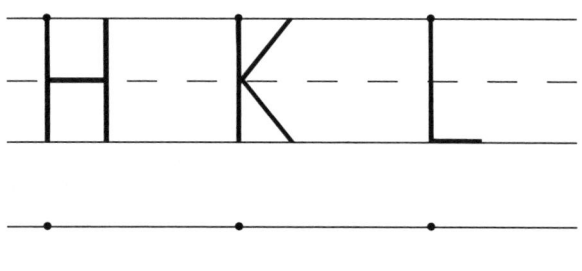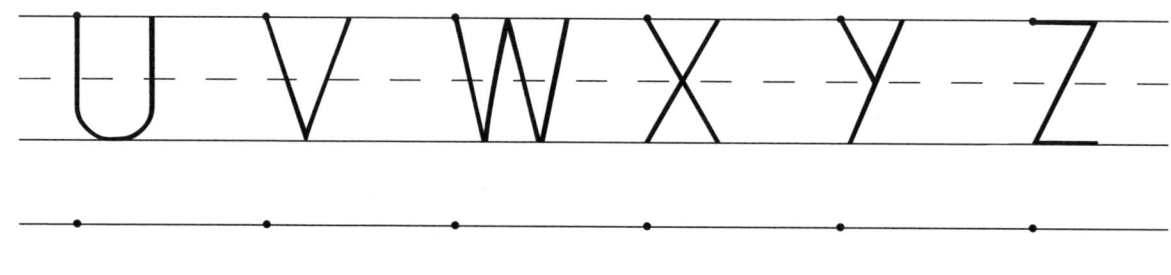

Start on the dot. Copy.

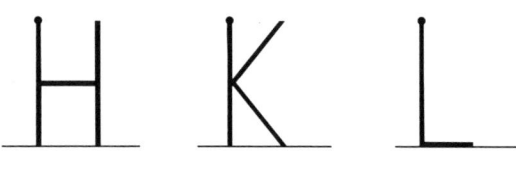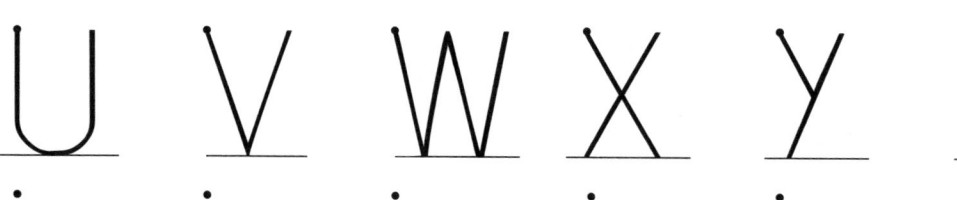

CENTER STARTING CAPITALS

C O Q G S A I T J are Center Starting Capitals.

Start with a Magic C. Copy.

 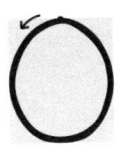 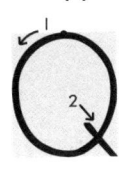 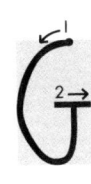

Start at the top in the center. Copy.

 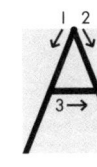  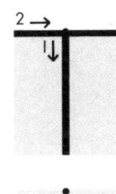 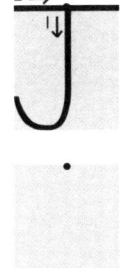

Start on the dot. Copy.

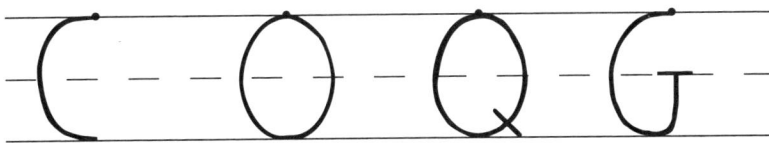   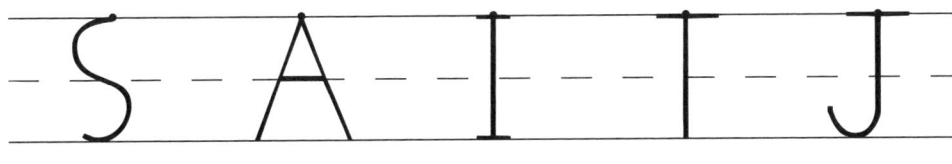

Start on the dot. Copy.

My Printing Book

CAPITAL REVIEW

Start on the dot. Copy the capitals.

A B C D E F G H

I J K L M N O P Q

R S T U V W X Y Z

NUMBER REVIEW

Start on the dot. Copy the numbers.

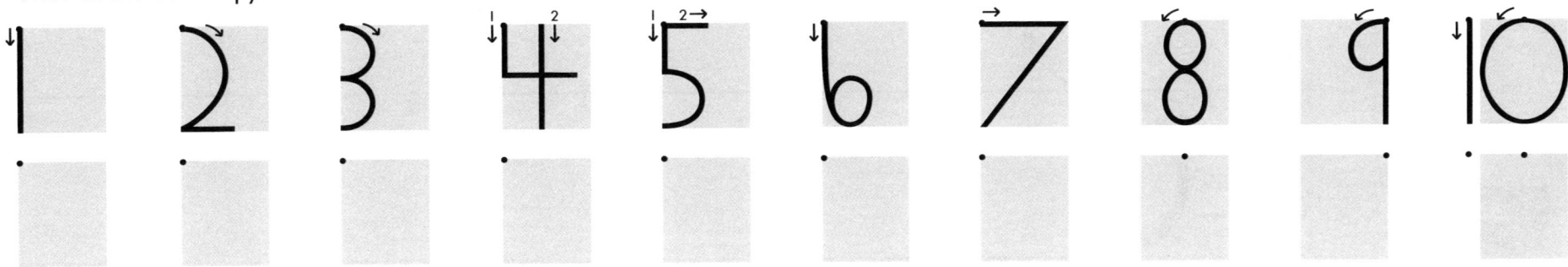

Teachers: Use these Gray Blocks for demonstration or student practice.

Start on the dot. Copy the numbers.

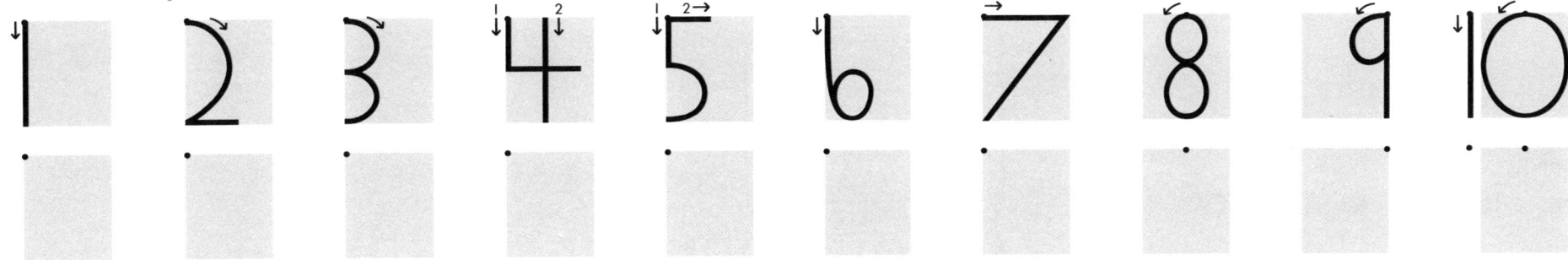

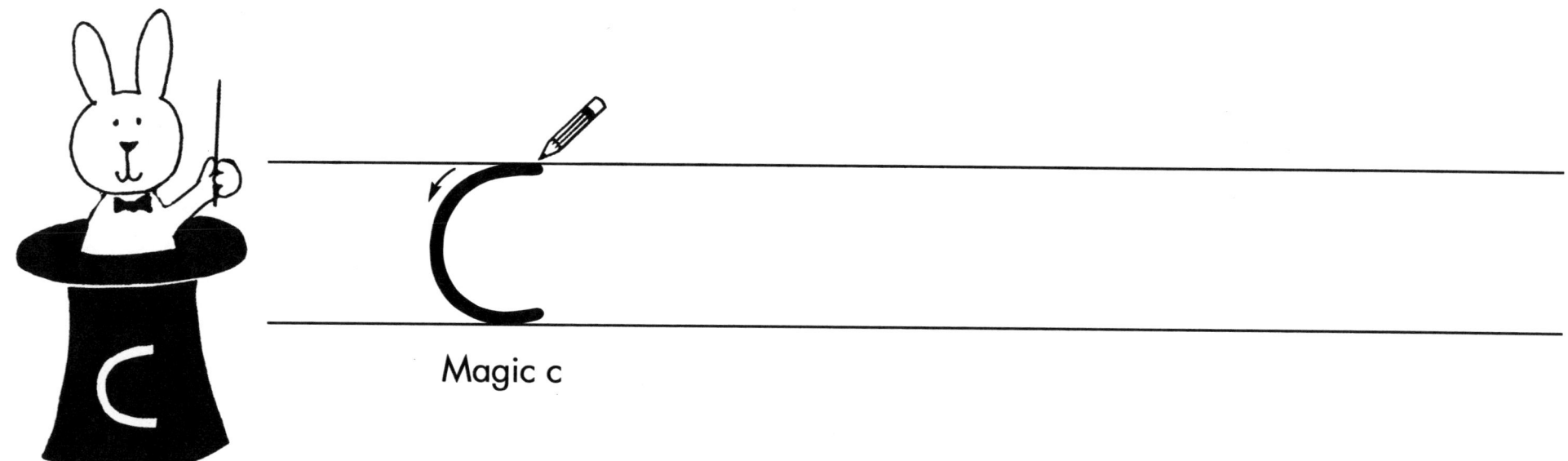

Magic c

Start on the dot. Copy c.

☐ Check c

c is for computer.

☑ Check letter. Teachers: Help children ✔ their letter for correct start, steps, and bump.

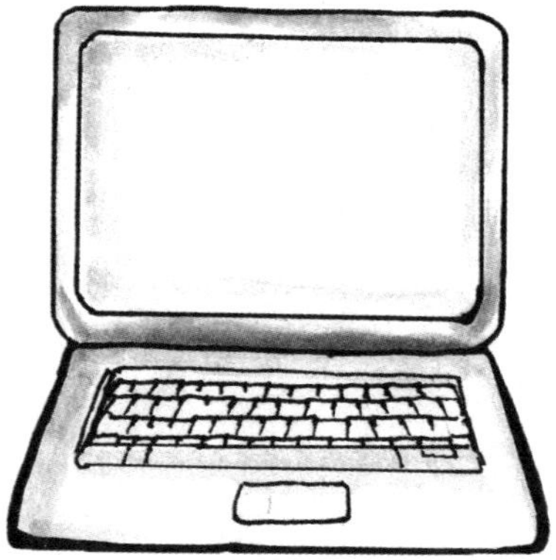

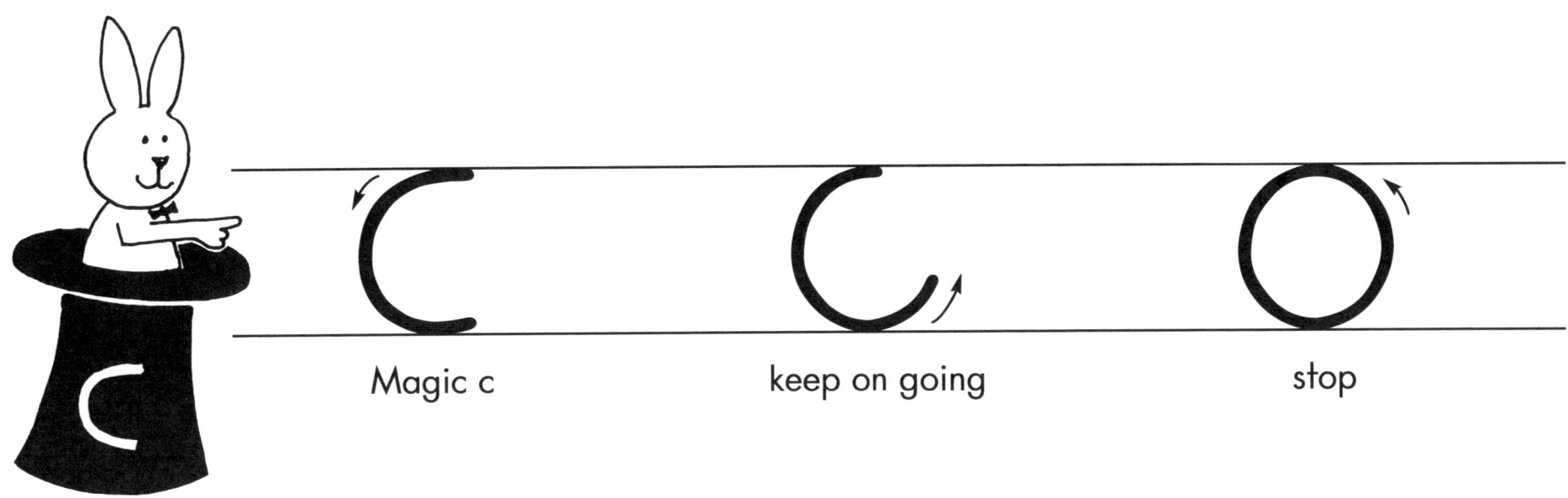

Magic c keep on going stop

Start on the dot. Copy O. ☐ Check O

O is for **o**ct**o**pus.

little Magic c

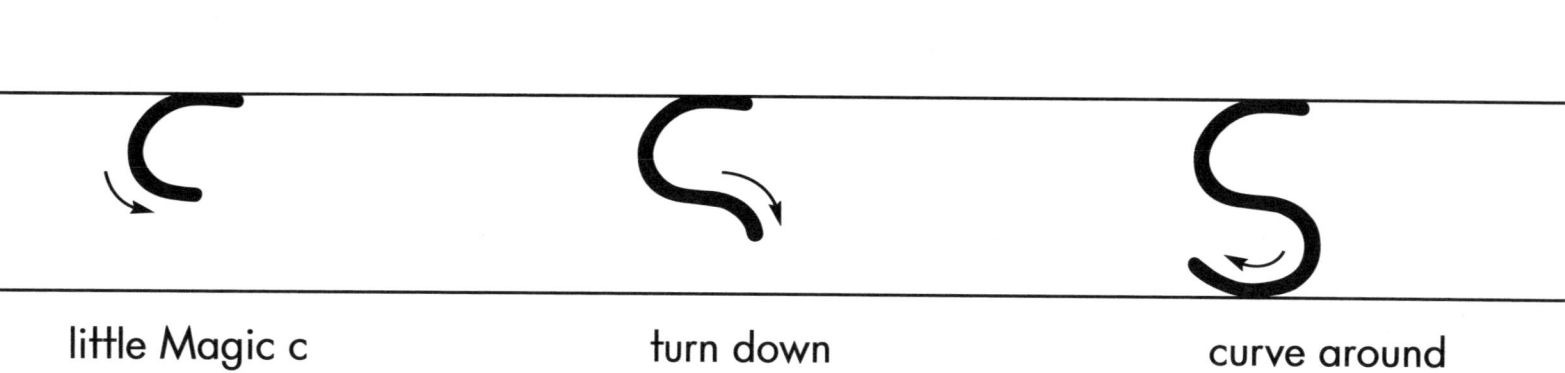

little Magic c   turn down   curve around

Start on the dot. Copy s.   ☑ Check s

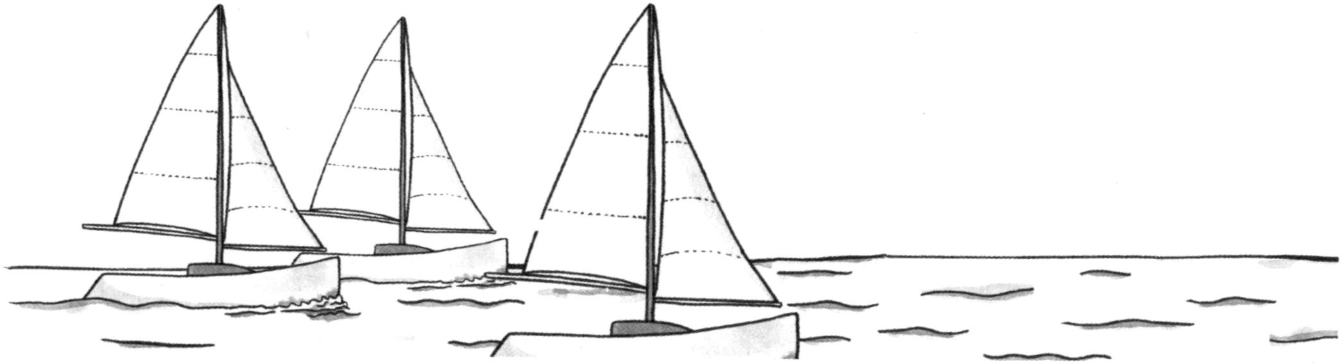

s is for sailboats.

PLURALS - ADD s

Start on the dot. Add s to make the words plural.

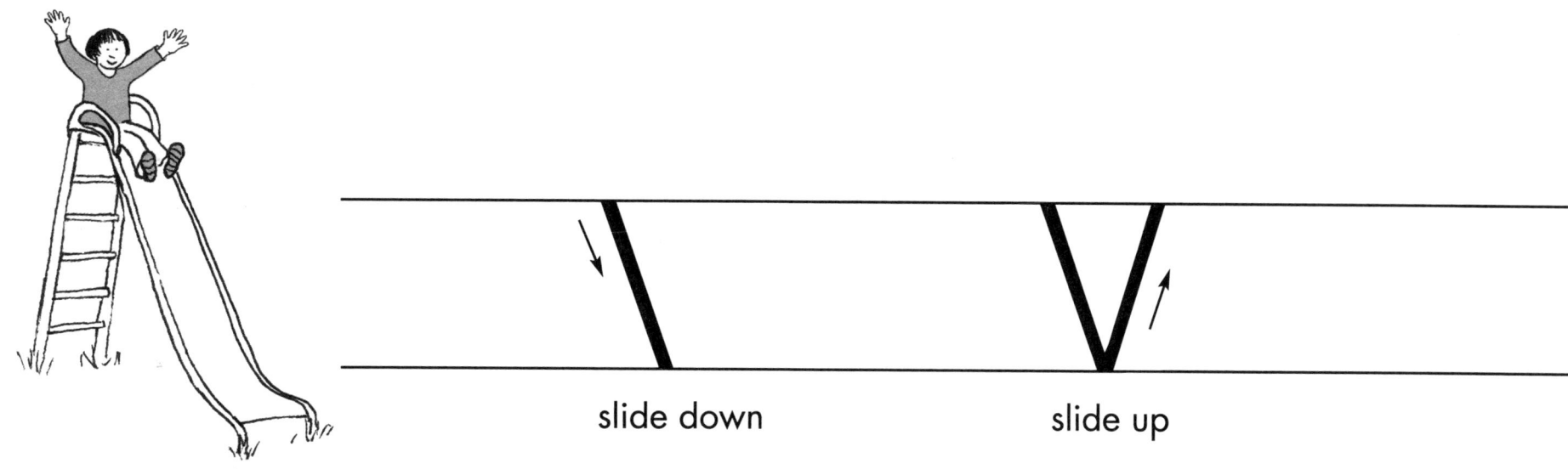

slide down   slide up

Start on the dot. Copy V.   ☐ Check V

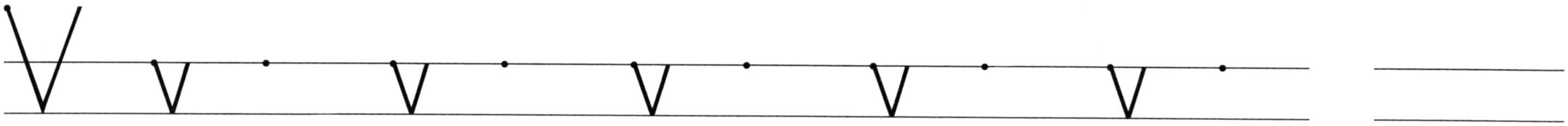

V is for vulture.

slide down and up   slide down and up

Start on the dot. Copy **W**.   ☐ Check **W**

W is for **w**alrus.

"Start at the top!"

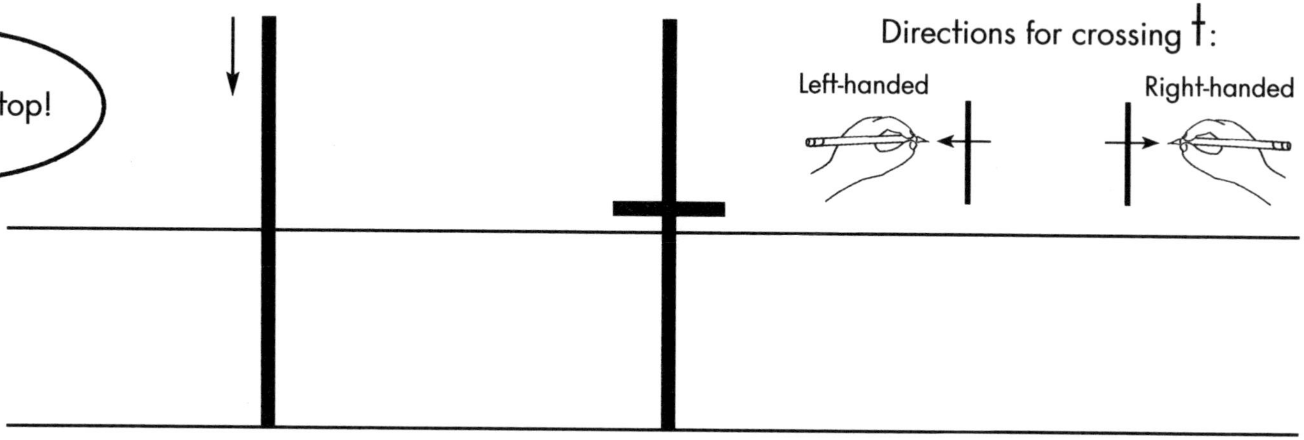

Directions for crossing t:
Left-handed   Right-handed

down
bump

cross

Start on the dot. Copy t.

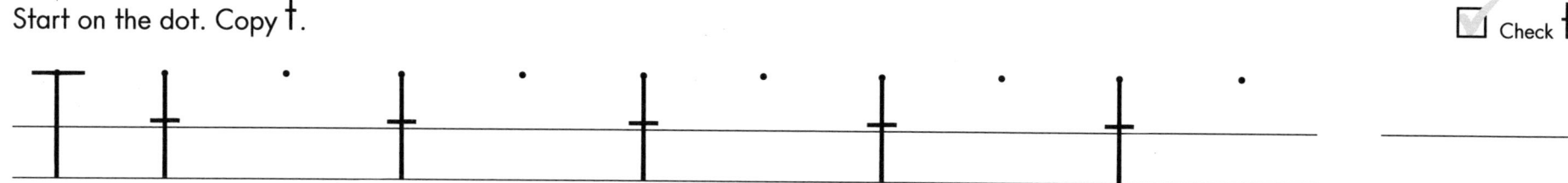

☑ Check t

T is for trumpet.

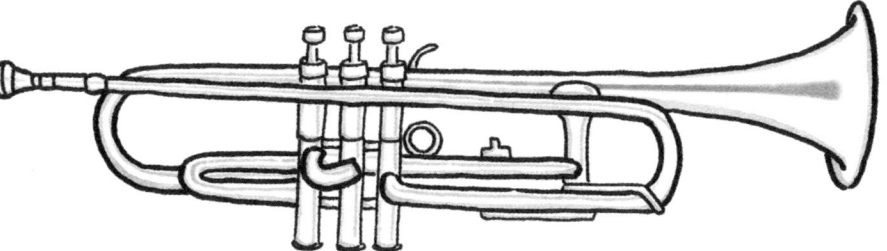

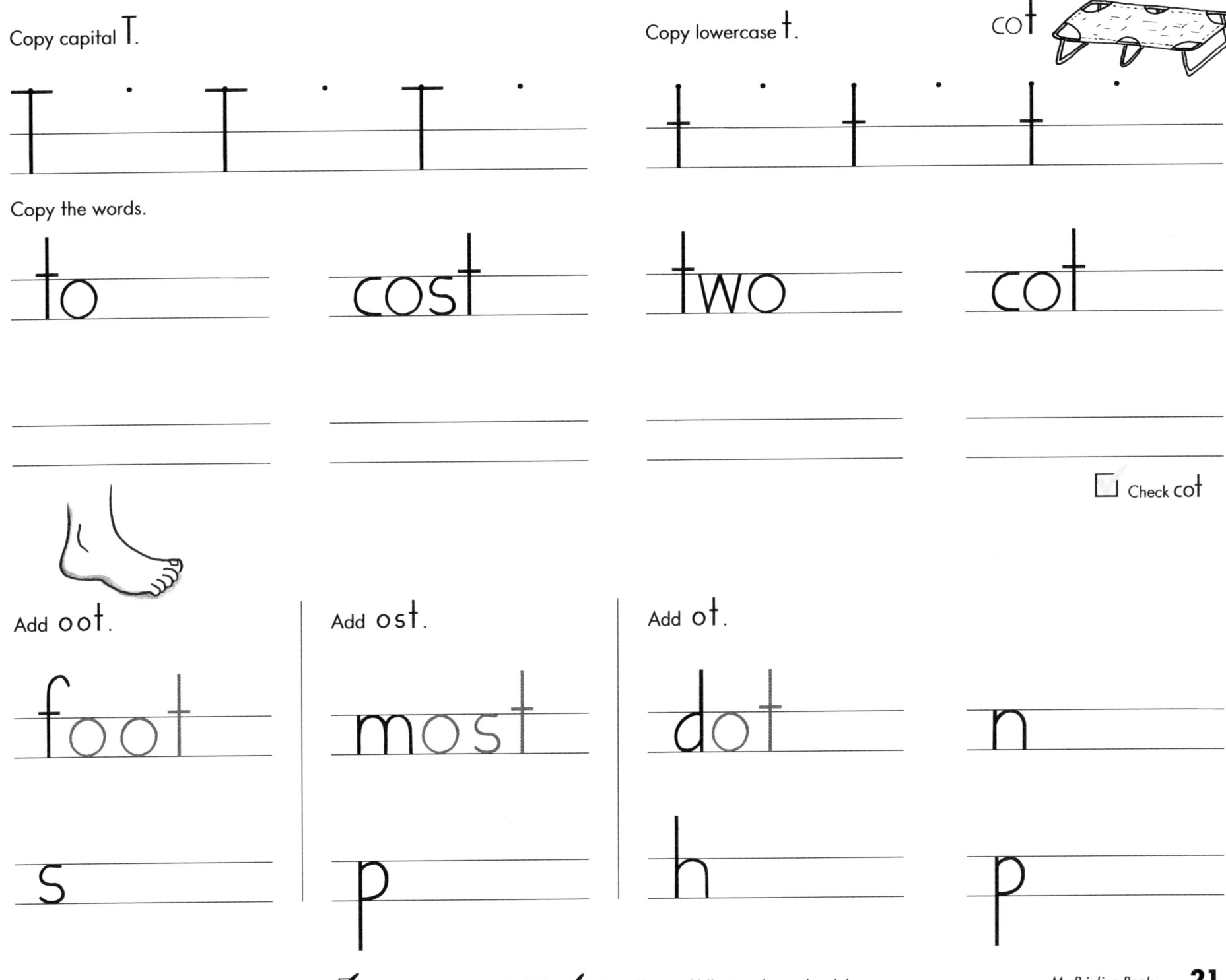

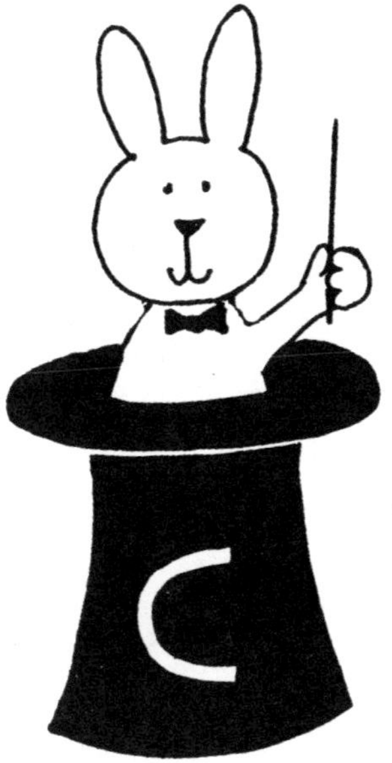

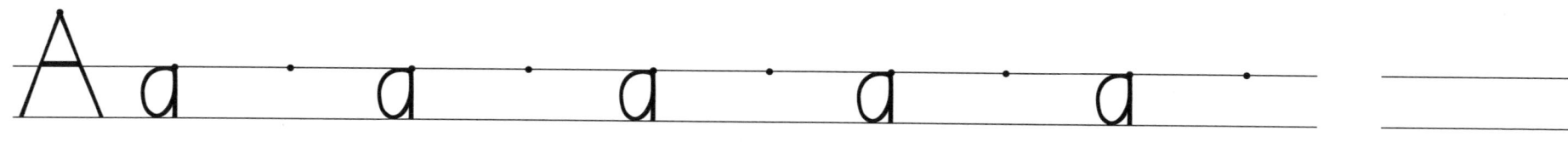

Magic c   up like a   bump   back down bump

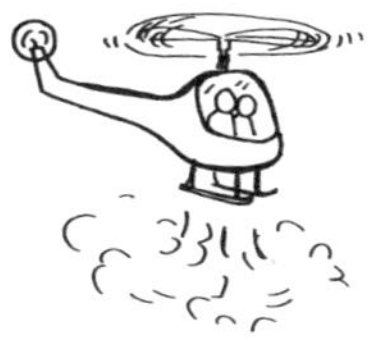

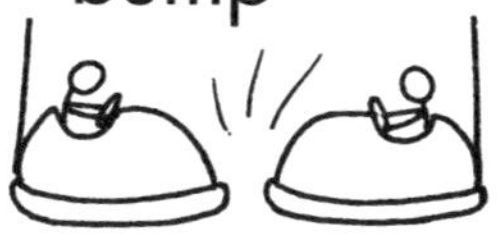

Start on the dot. Copy **a**.   ☑ Check **a**

A is for **a**stron**a**ut.

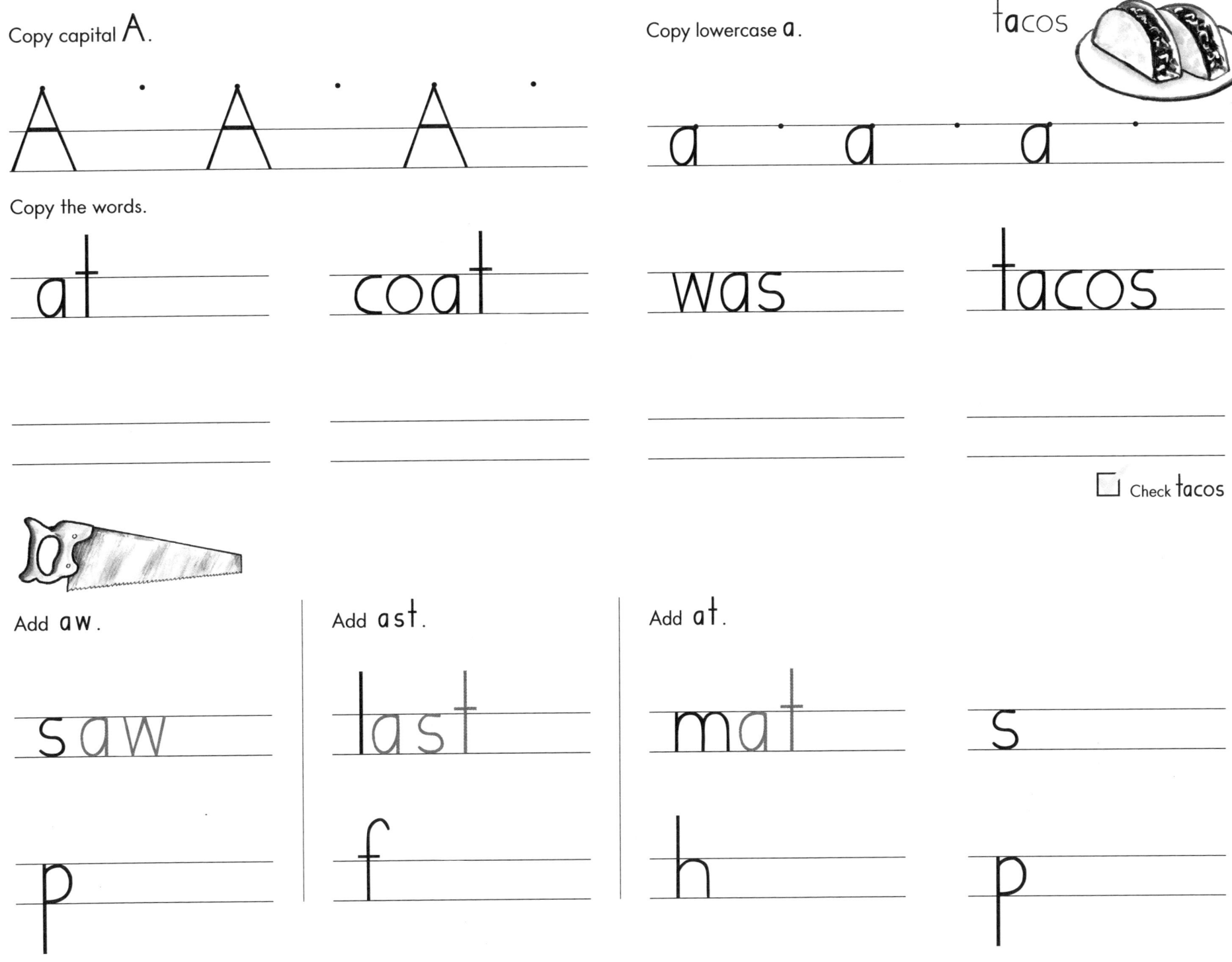

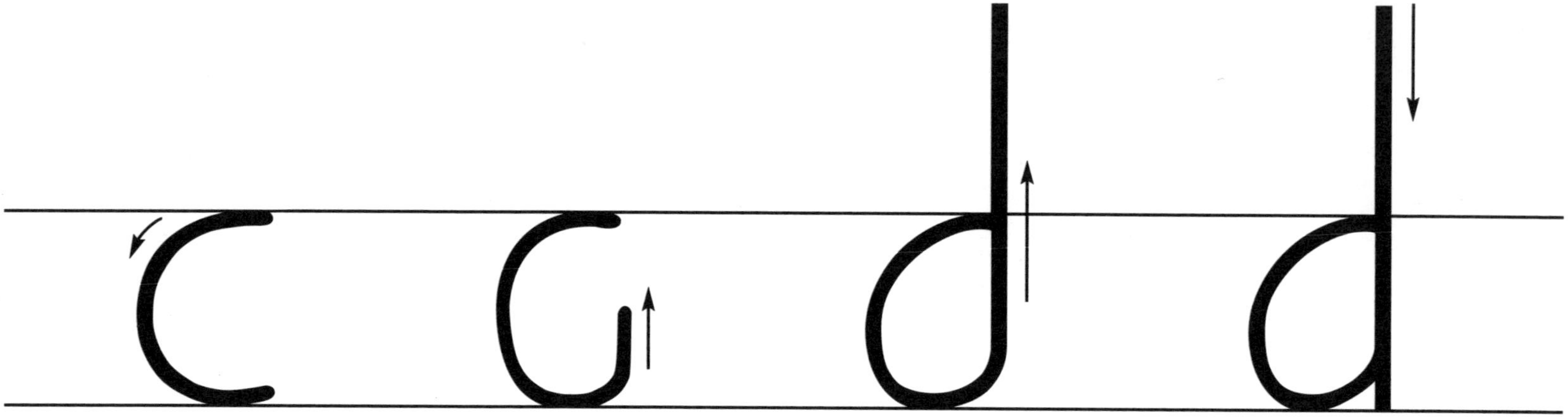

c c d d

Magic c   up like a   up higher   back down bump

Start on the dot. Copy d.   ☑ Check d

D d · d · d · d · d

D is for **d**ragon.

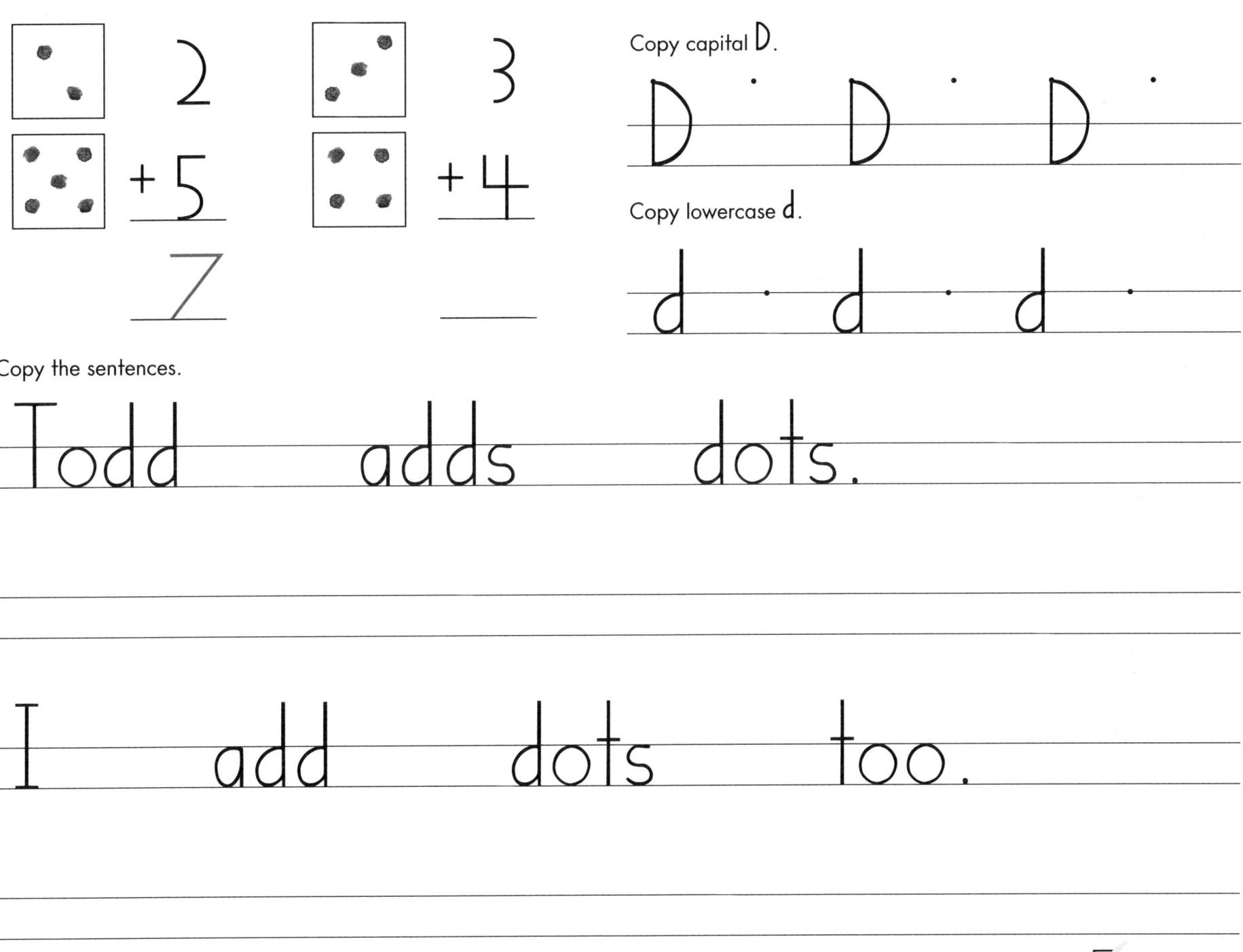

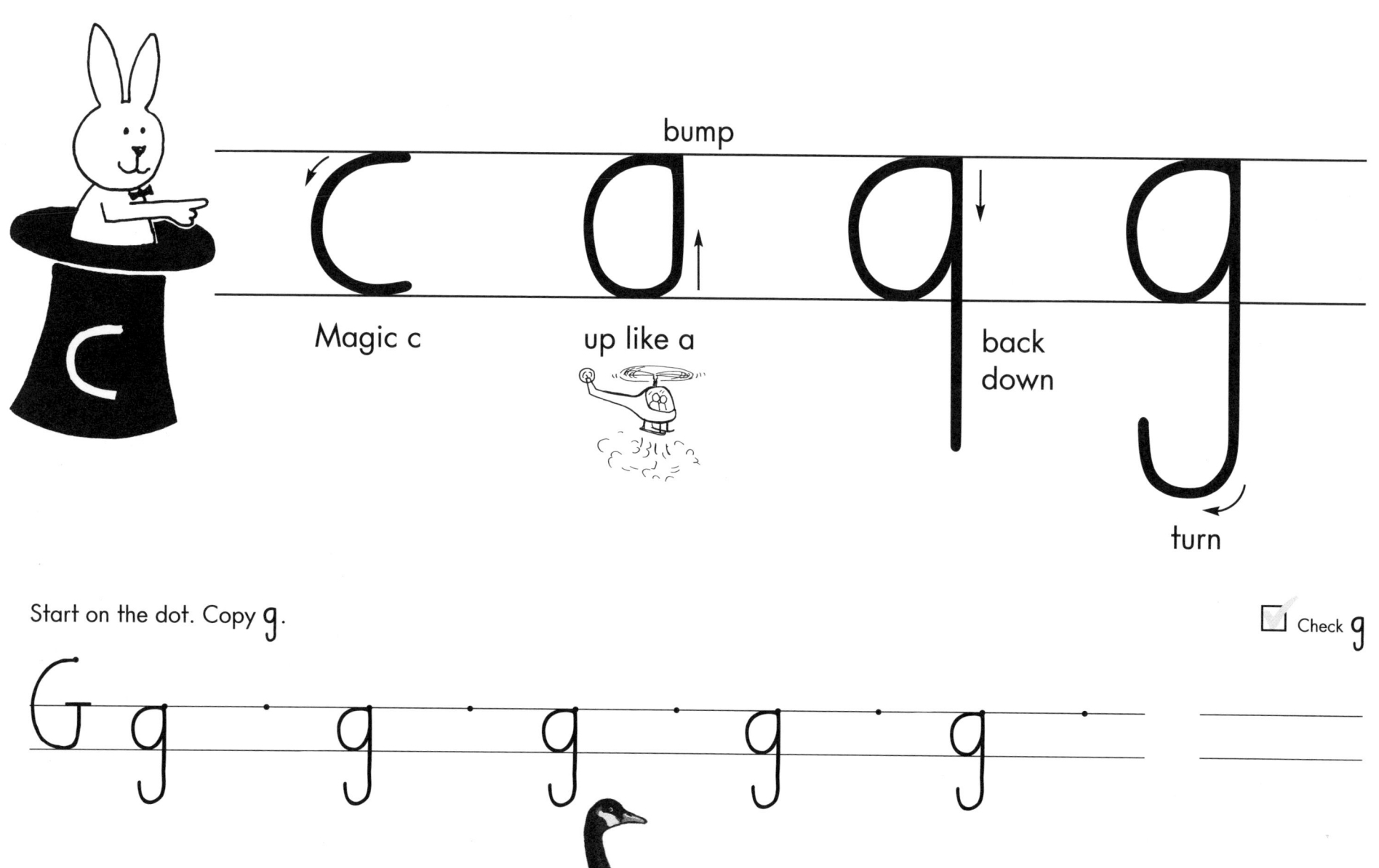

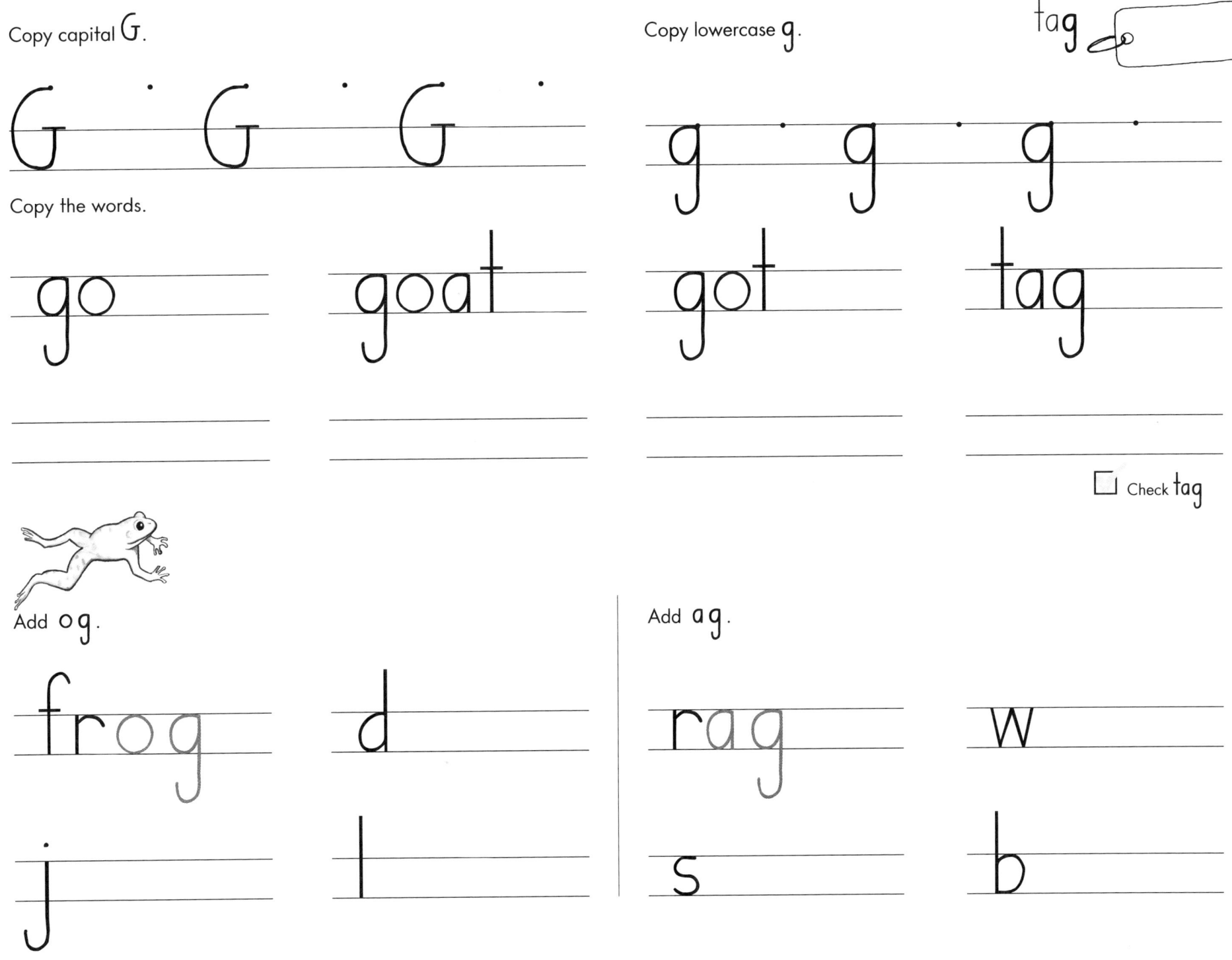

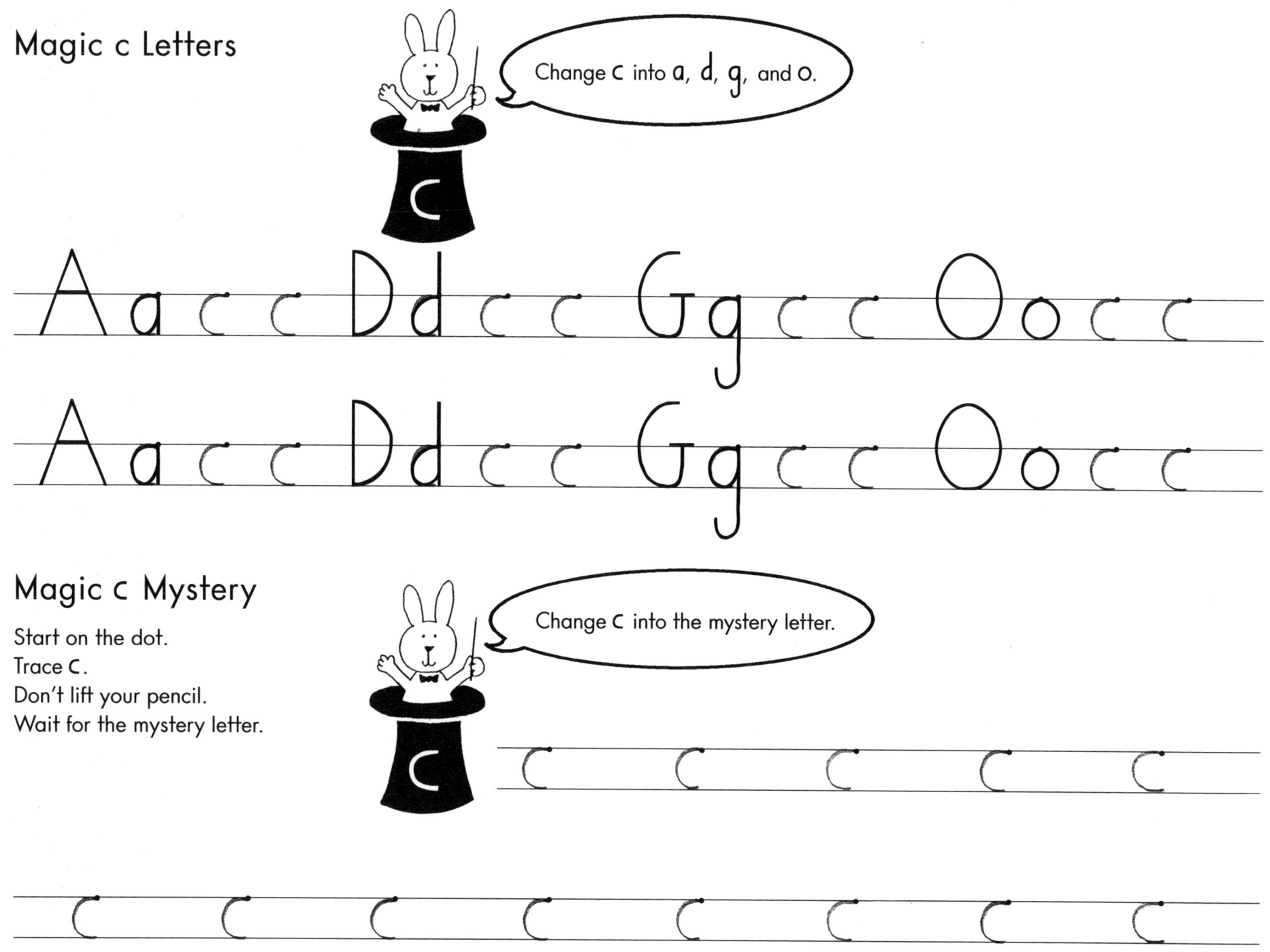

The Hand Activity

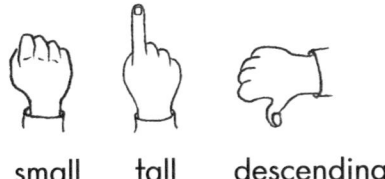
small tall descending

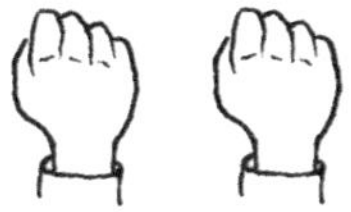

Copy.

on   cow    at 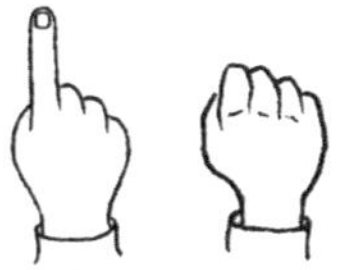   do

go

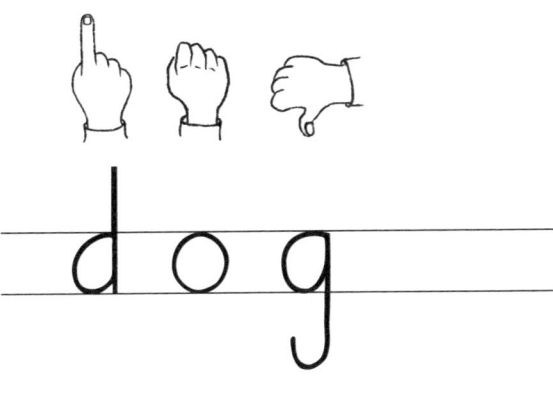
dog

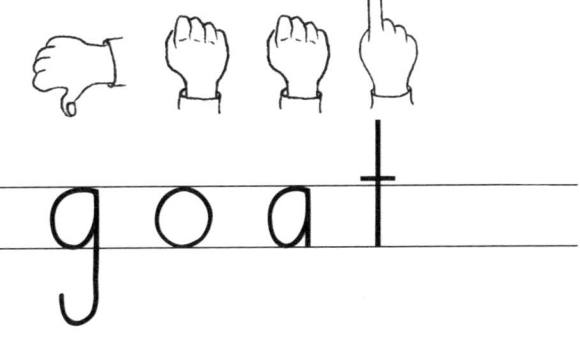
goat

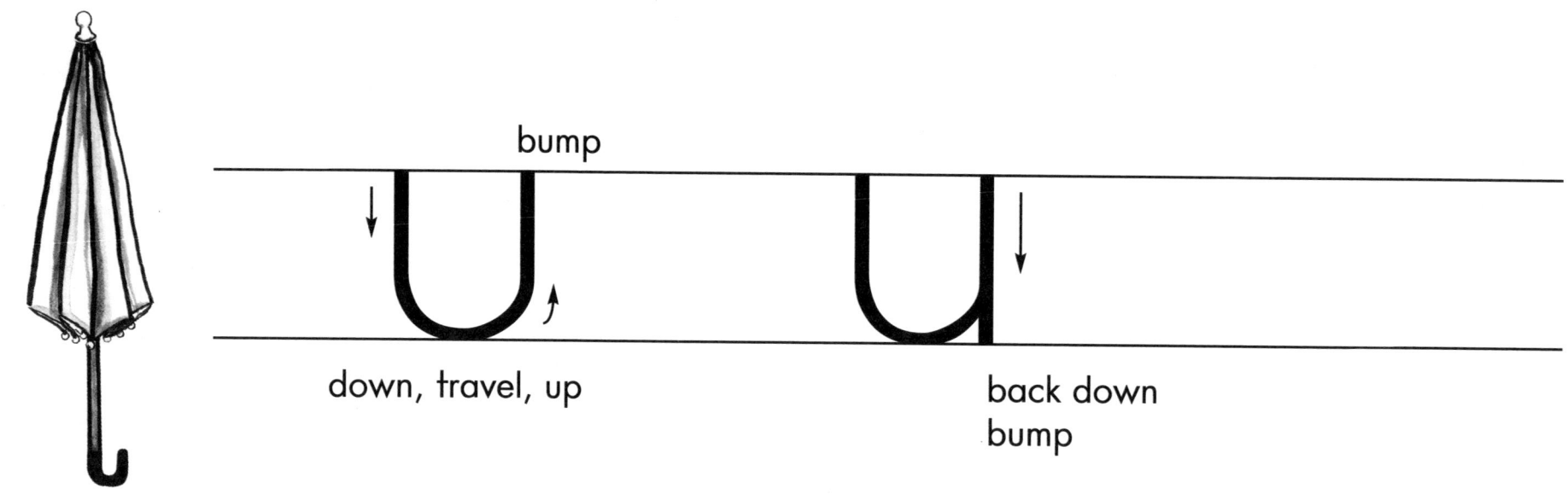

bump
down, travel, up
back down bump

Start on the dot. Copy u.

☑ Check u

U is for ukulele.

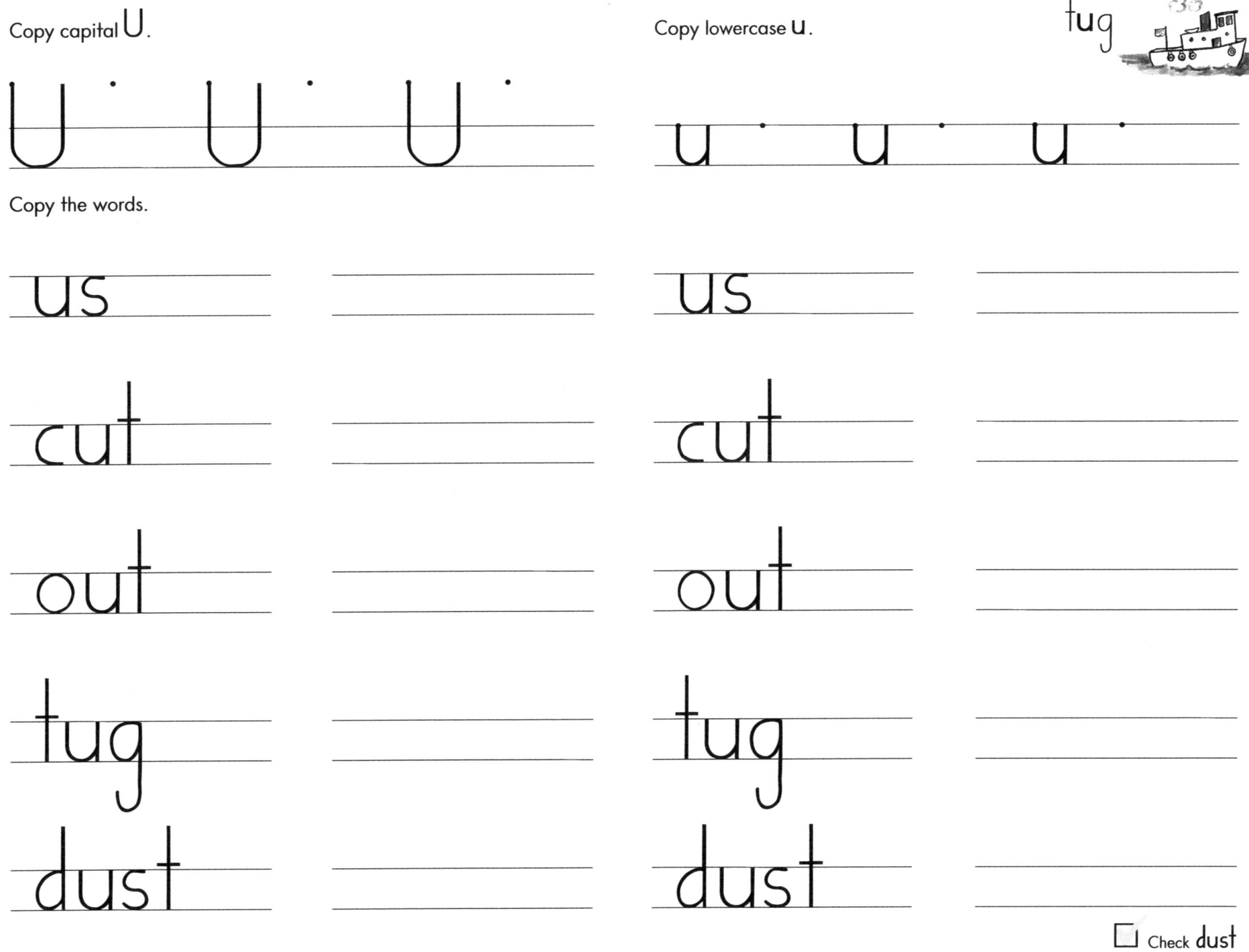

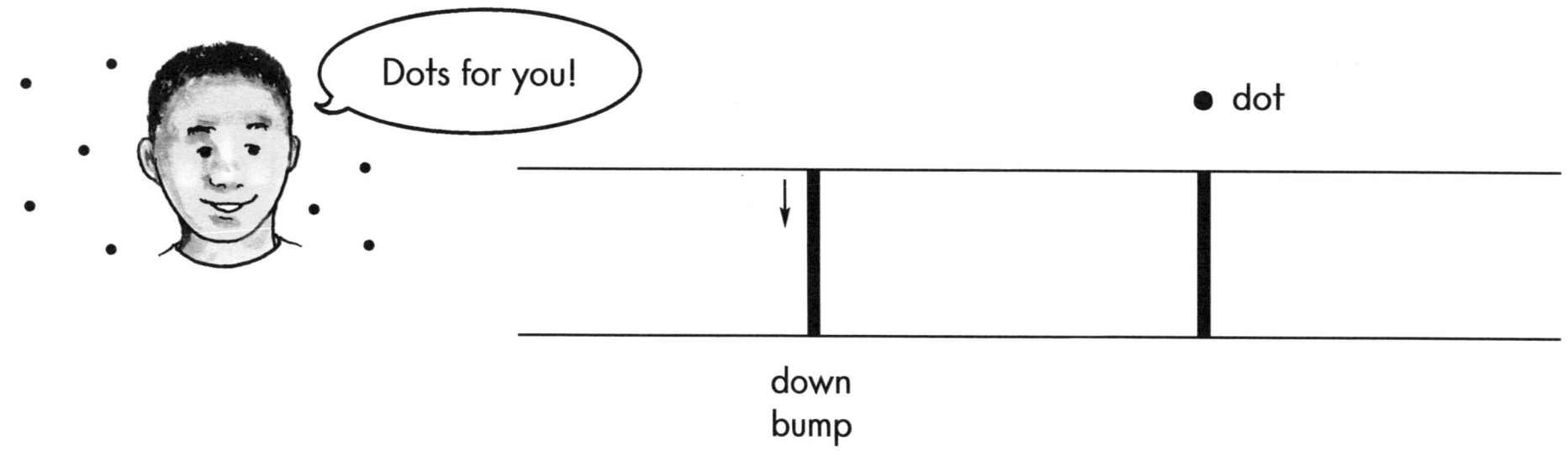

Start on the dot. Copy i.   ☑ Check i

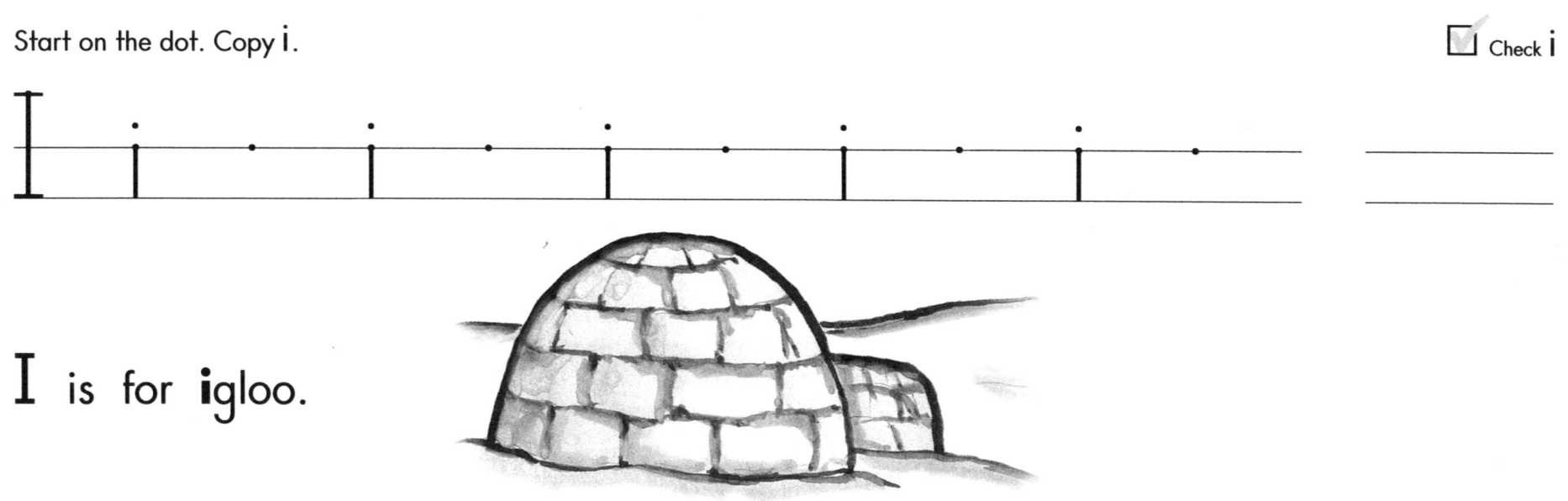

I is for igloo.

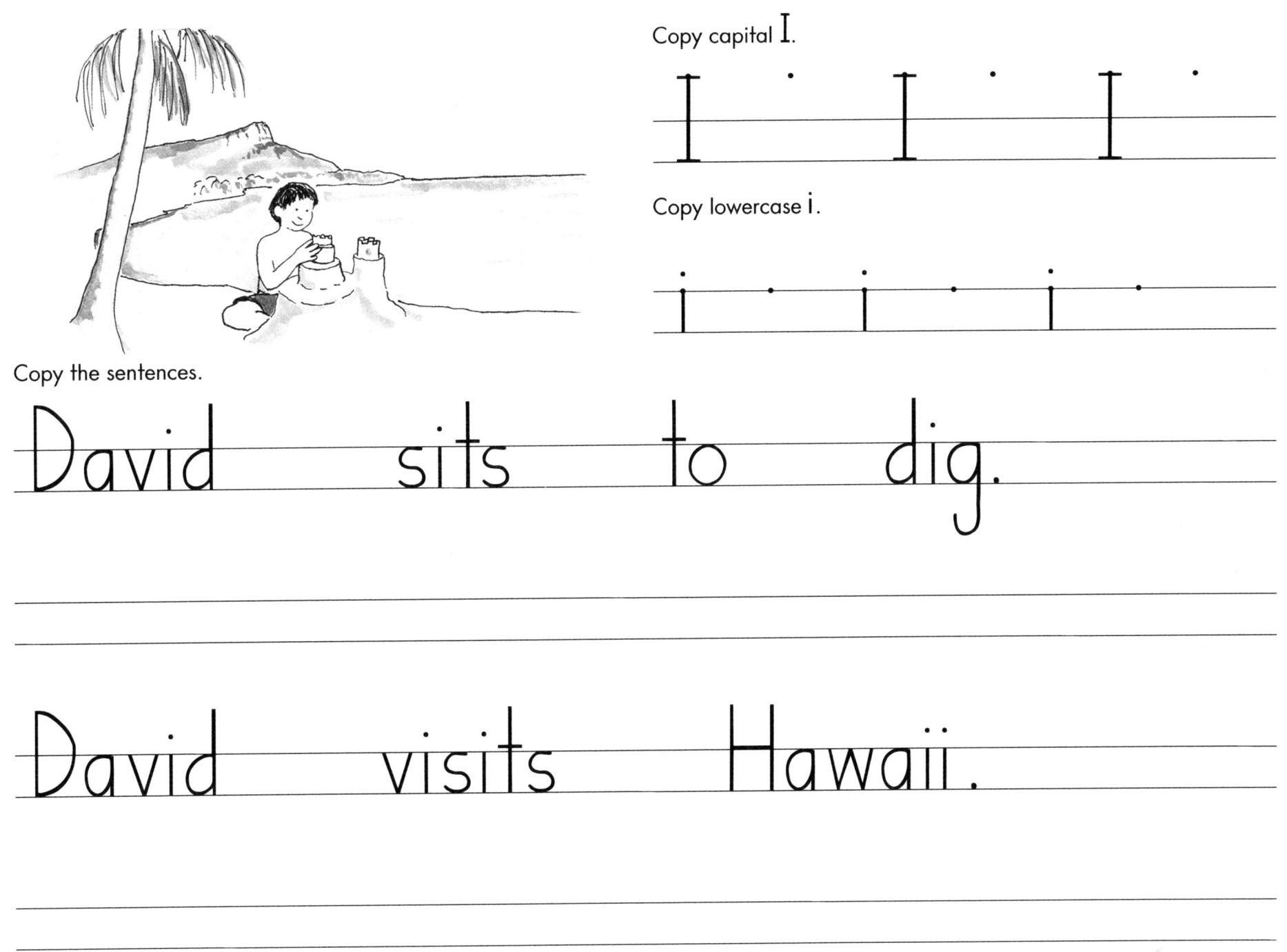

Copy capital I.

Copy lowercase i.

Copy the sentences.

David sits to dig.

David visits Hawaii.

☐ Check Sentence

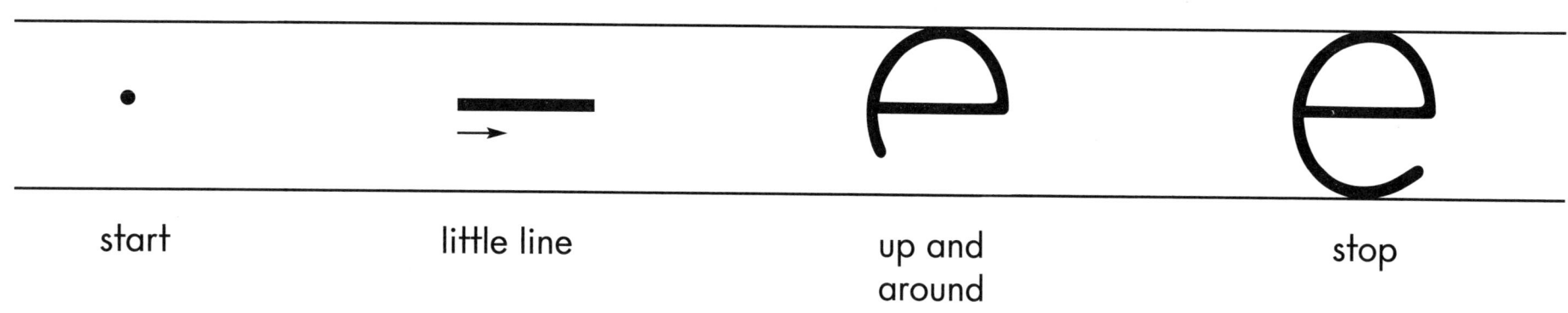

| start | little line | up and around | stop |

Start on the dot. Copy e. Check e

E e · e · e · e · e ·

E is for **e**agl**e**.

Copy capital **E**.

E · E · E ·

Copy lowercase **e**.

seed

e · e · e ·

Copy the words.

eat   give   gave   seed

☐ Check **seed**

Add **est**.

nest
b

Add **eed**.

need
f

Add **et**.

met   l
g   n

My Printing Book **35**

RHYMES

Copy the rhymes.

two - dew   goat - coat

—   —

cage - wage   toe - go

—   —

PUNCTUATION

Copy the punctuation marks.

. .	? ?	! !
Periods	Question marks	Exclamation points
. .	? ?	! !

Copy the sentences.

Do we eat tacos? We do.

Tacos taste so good!

"Start at the top!"

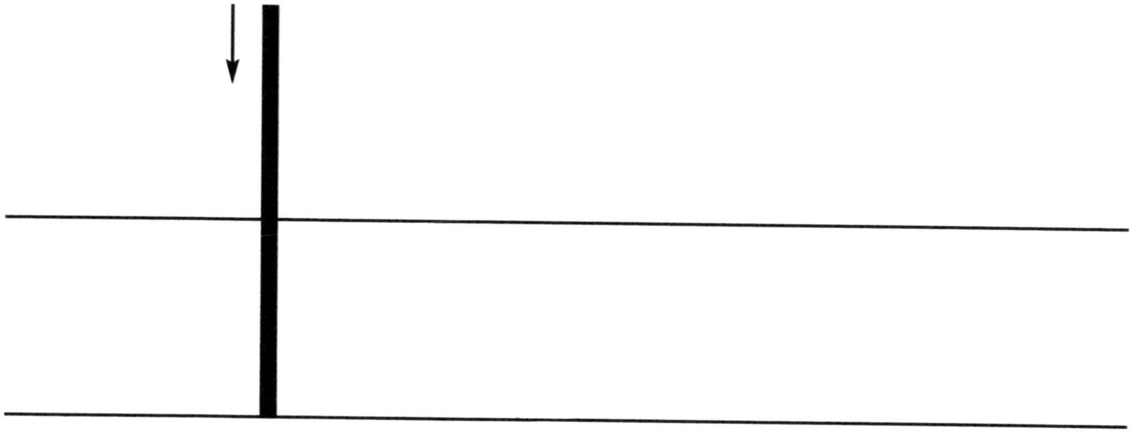

down
bump

Start on the dot. Copy l. Check l

L is for lobster.

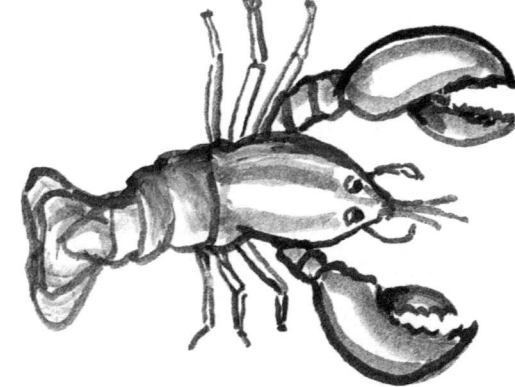

Copy capital L.

Copy lowercase l.

Copy the sentences.

We see a tall slide.

Ellie Sue will slide.

☐ Check Sentence

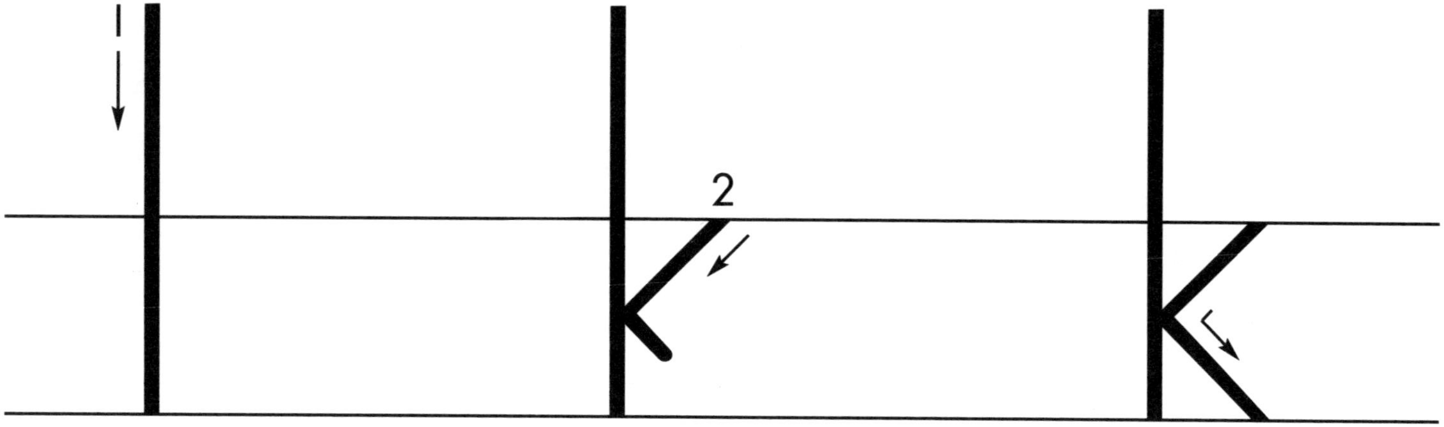

down bump	kick!	slide away

Start on the dot. Copy k.   ☑ Check k

K k k k k k

K is for **k**aya**k**.

Copy capital K.

K　K　K

Copy lowercase k.　kick

k　k　k

Copy the words.

kite　like　look　kick

☐ Check kick

Add oot.

boot

r

Add ick.

sick

p

Add ake.

make　b

sh　t

My Printing Book　41

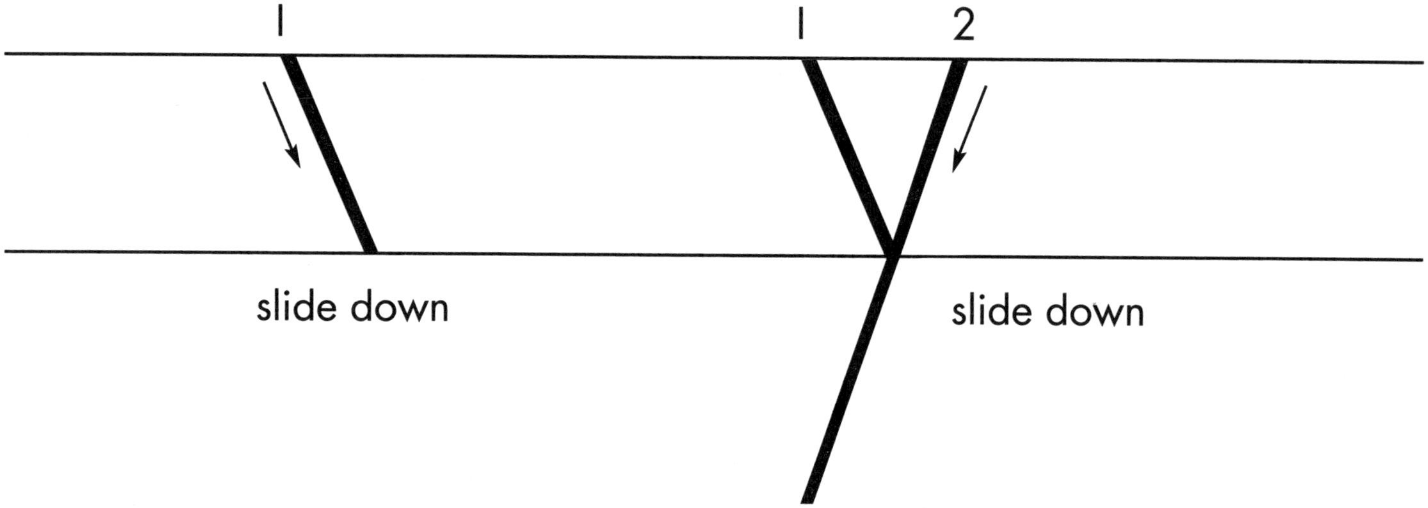

1   1 2
slide down   slide down

Start on the dot. Copy y.   ☑ Check y

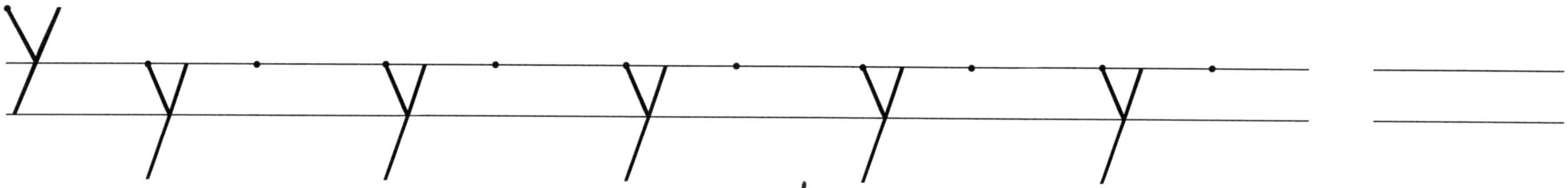

y is for yak.

Copy capital Y.

Y Y Y

Copy lowercase y.

y y y

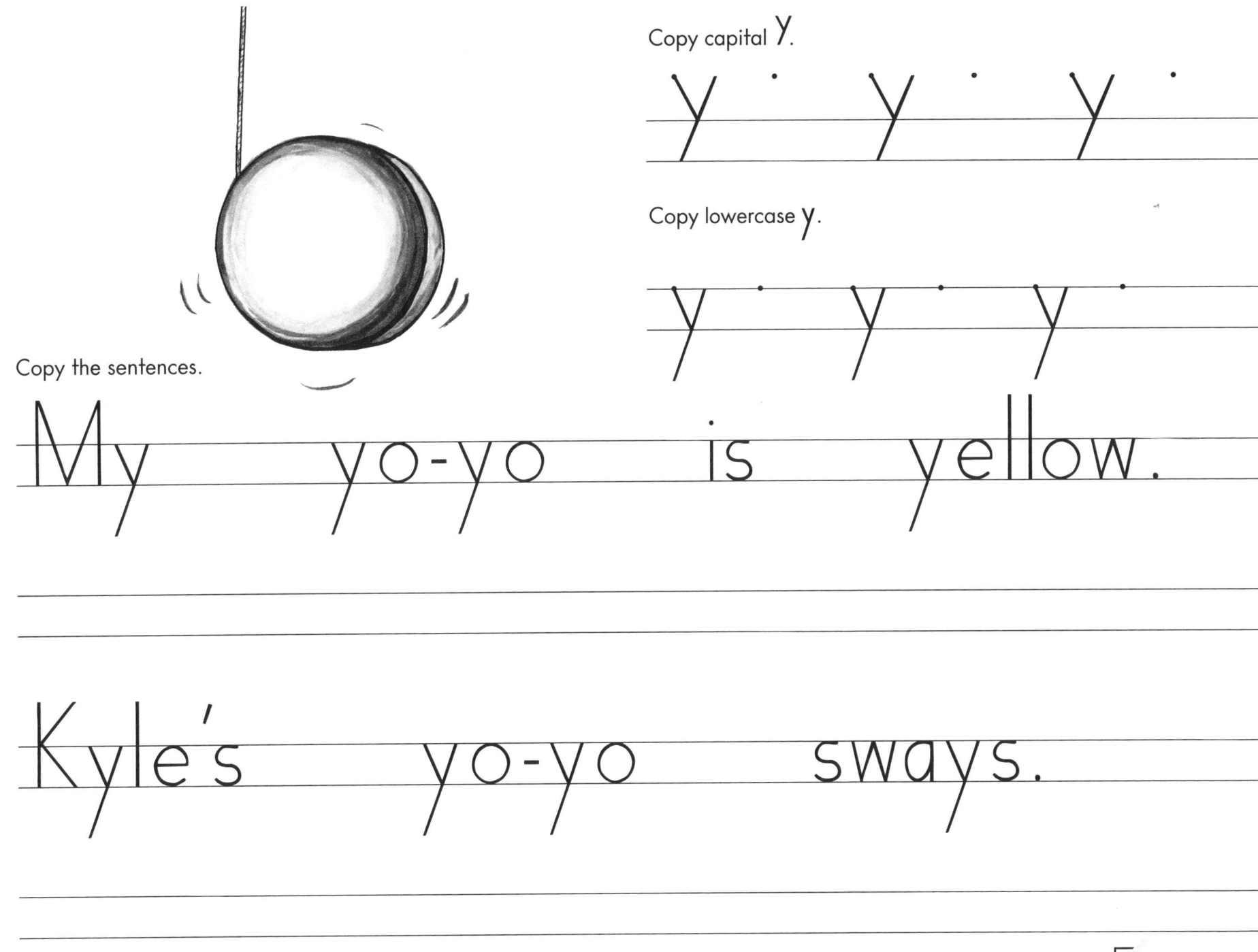

Copy the sentences.

My yo-yo is yellow.

Kyle's yo-yo sways.

☐ Check Sentence

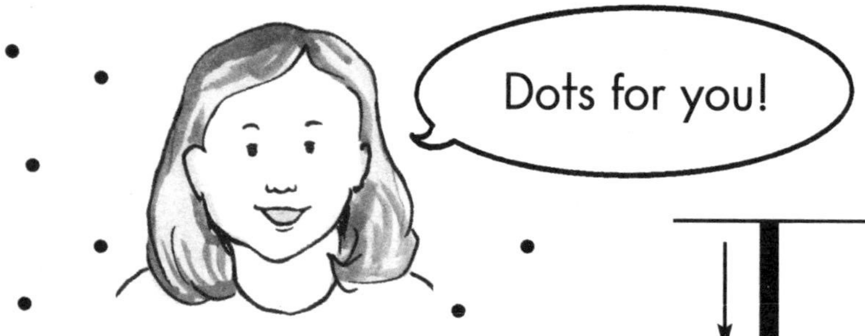

Dots for you!

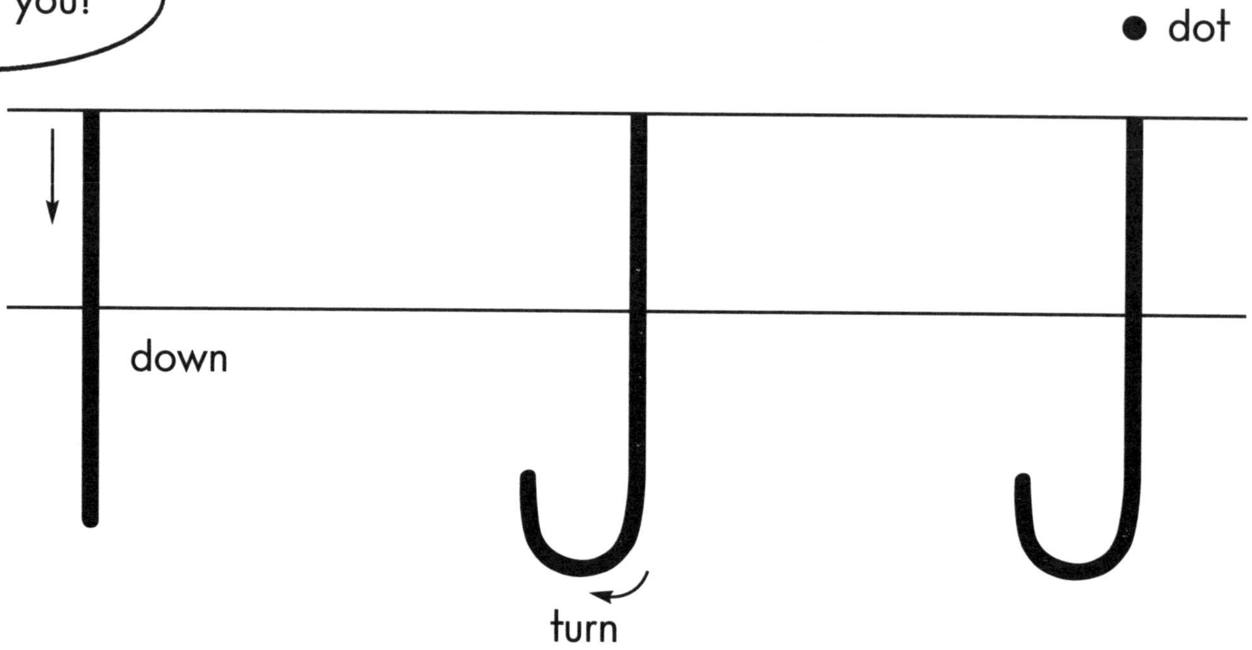

• dot

↓
down

turn

Start on the dot. Copy j. ☑ Check j

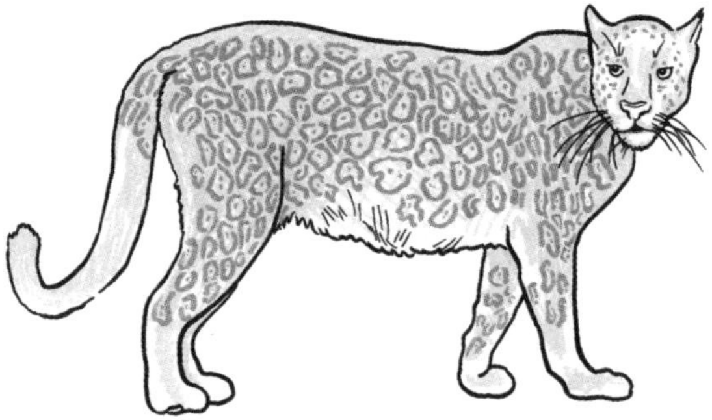

J is for jaguar.

Copy capital J.

J   J   J

Copy the words.

jet

joke

just

Jack

July

Copy lowercase j.   jet

j   j   j

jet

joke

just

Jack

July

☐ Check July

My Printing Book

MAGIC c SILLY SPELLING WORDS

Wait for your teacher to spell the words. Write the words on double lines.

You can make words with Magic C. Trace C and wait for your teacher.

Wait for your teacher to spell the words. Write the words on triple lines.

Wait for your teacher to spell the words. Write the words on single lines.

Teachers: See teacher's guide for examples.

LINE PRACTICE
Copy the sentence on double lines.

Zack saw two cats.

Copy the sentence on triple lines.

Ava saw two goats.

Copy the sentence on a single line.

Josie saw two dogs.

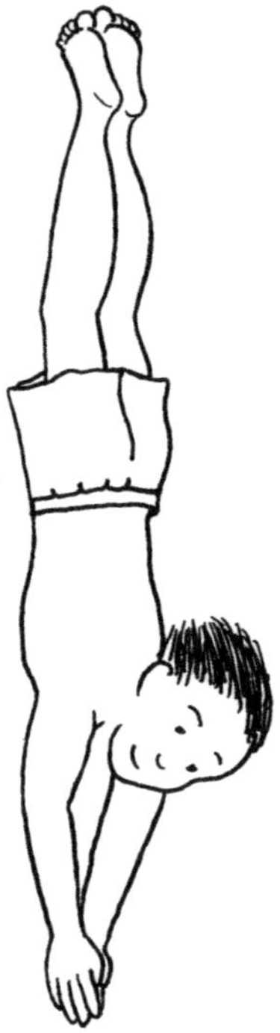

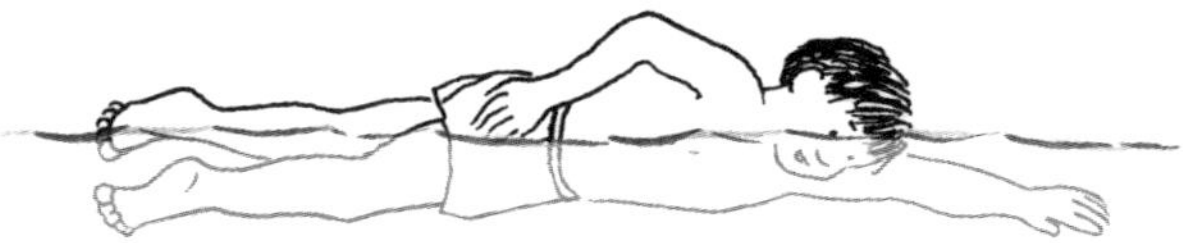

dive down

swim up
and over

around
bump

Start on the dot. Copy p.

Check p

p p p p p p

p is for **p**laty**p**us.

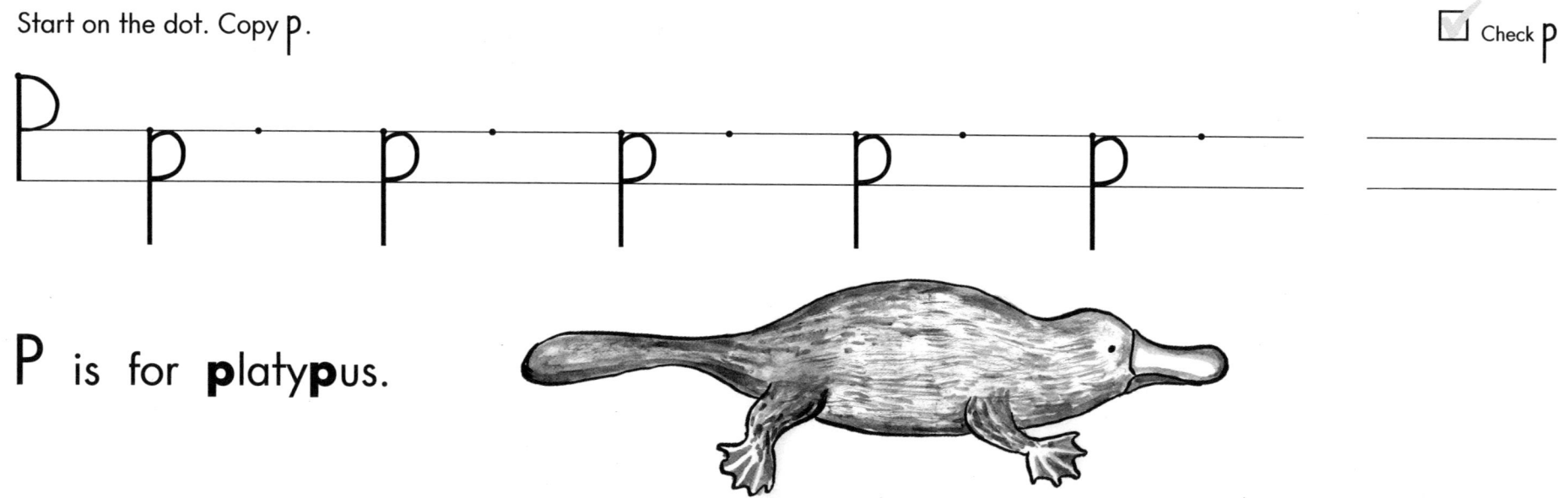

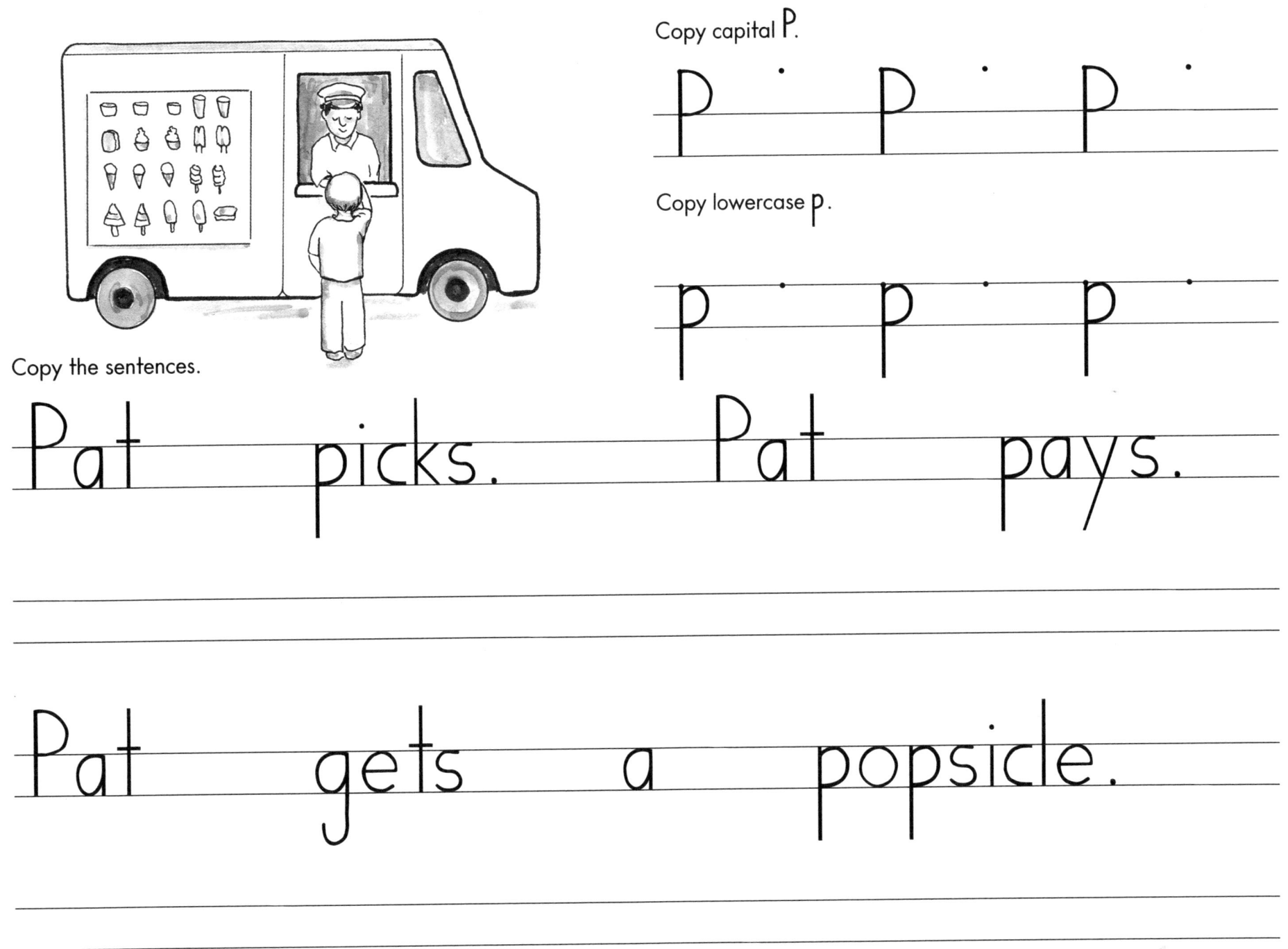

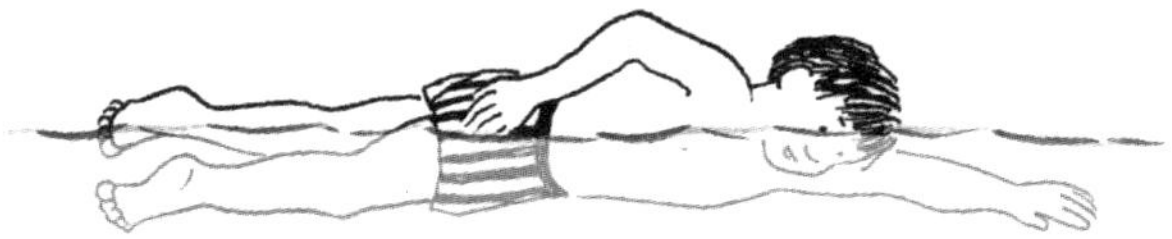

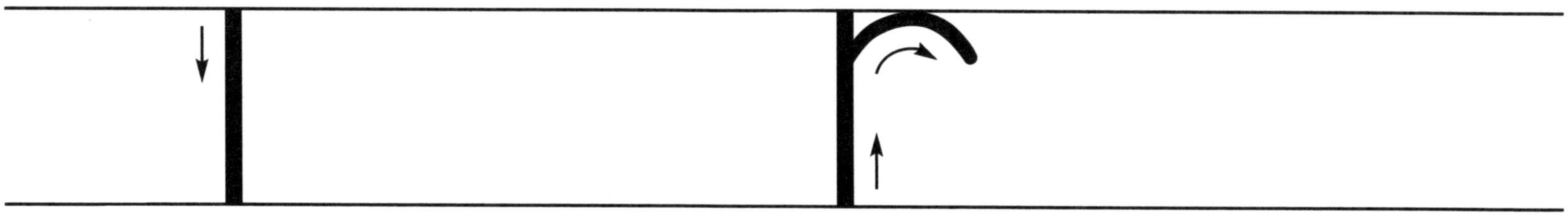

dive down

swim up
and over

Start on the dot. Copy r. ☐ Check r

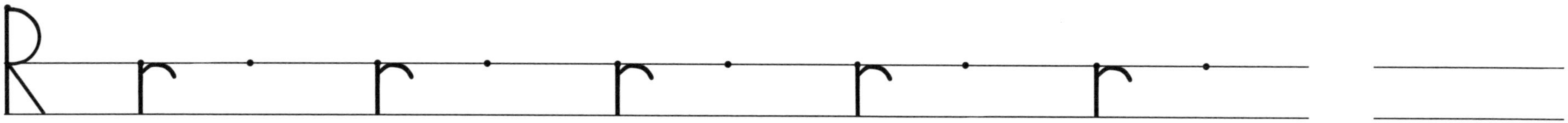

R r r r r r

R is for rowboat.

50 My Printing Book

© 2022 Learning Without Tears

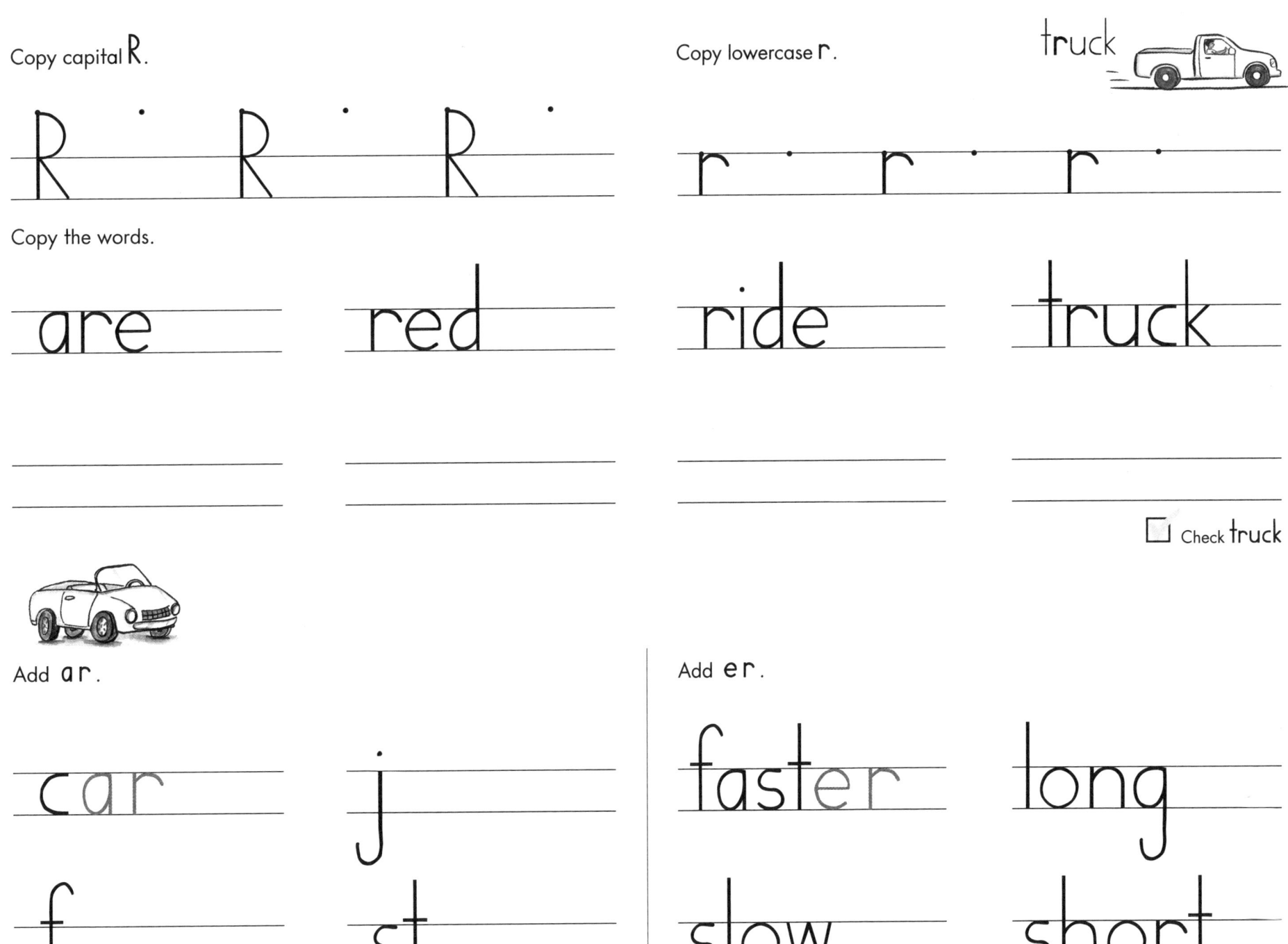

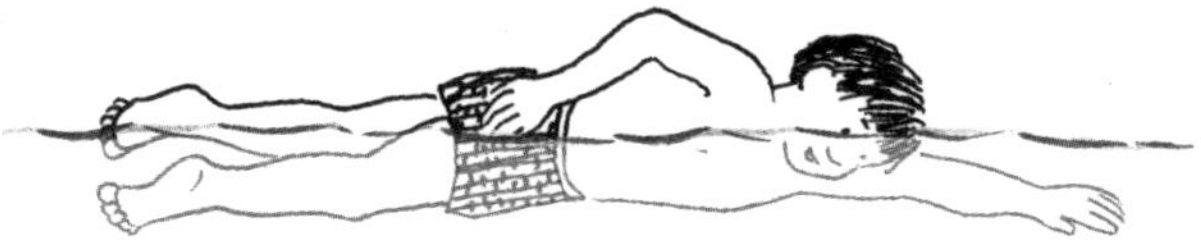

dive down swim up and over down

Start on the dot. Copy n.   ☑ Check n

N n . n . n . n . n .

N is for nickels.

My Printing Book © 2022 Learning Without Tears

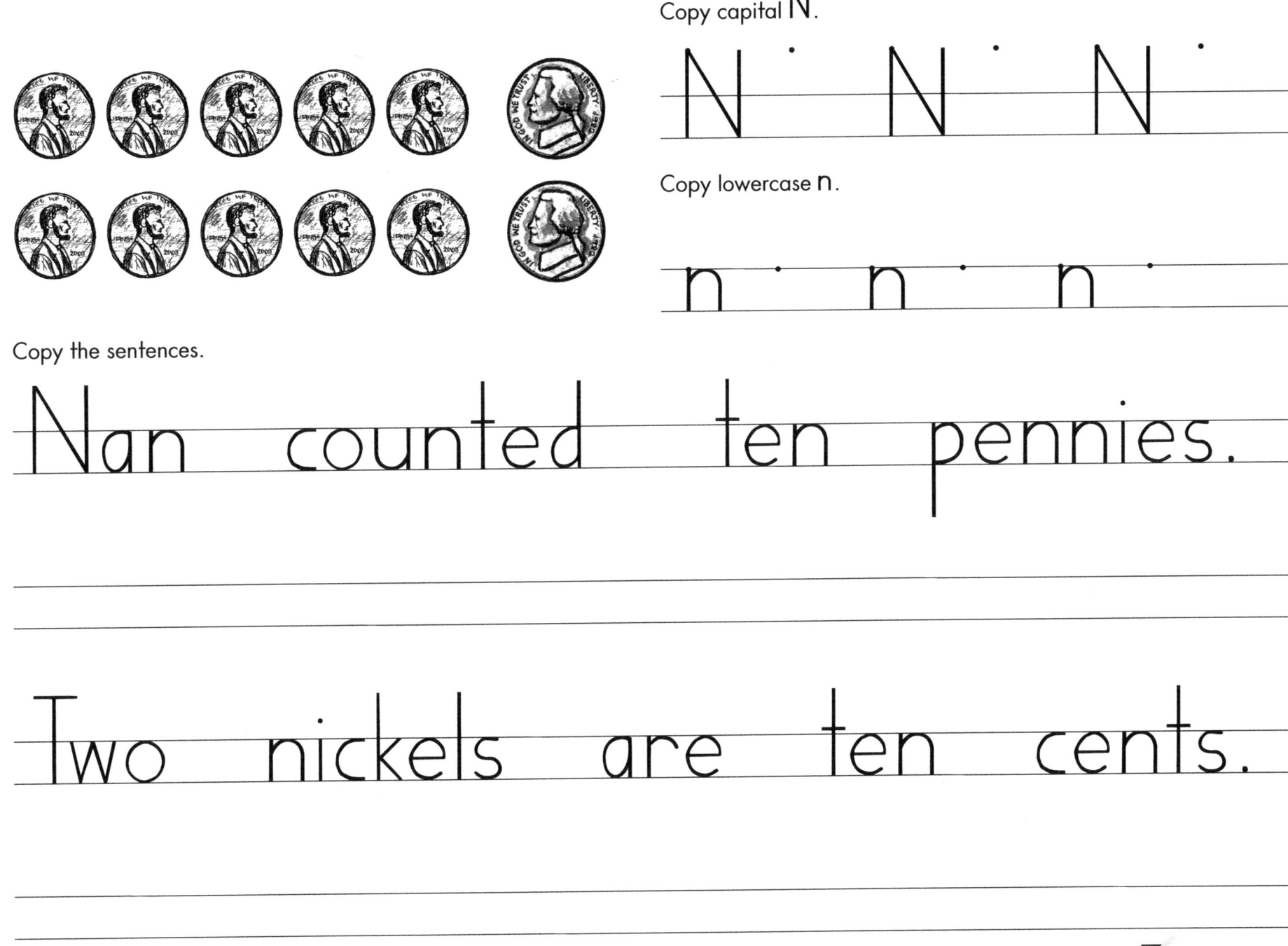

Copy capital N.

Copy lowercase n.

Copy the sentences.

Nan counted ten pennies.

Two nickels are ten cents.

☐ Check Sentence

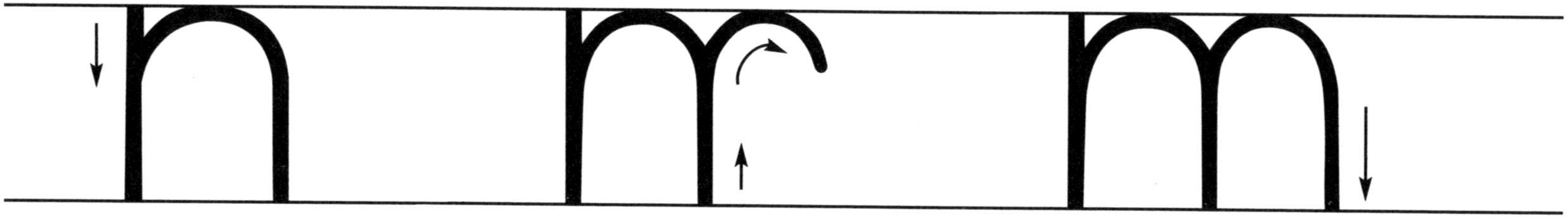

n m m

start with n | swim up and over | down

Start on the dot. Copy m. ☐ Check m

M m m m m m

M is for moose.

Copy capital M.

M M M

Copy lowercase m.

m m m

moon

Copy the words.

make   made   my   moon

☐ Check moon

Add im.

swim

tr___

Add ime.

time

d___

Add ame.

came

s___   t___
       f___

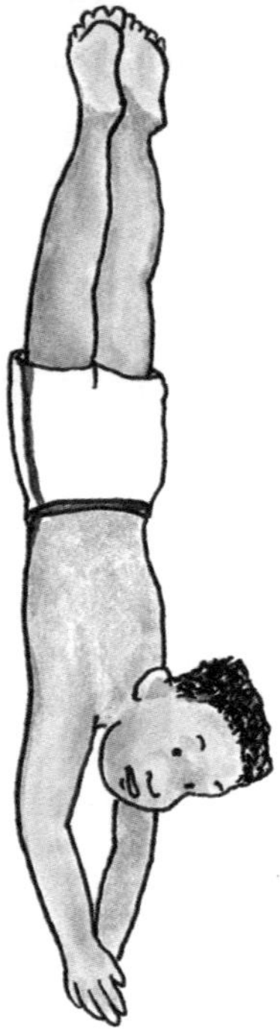

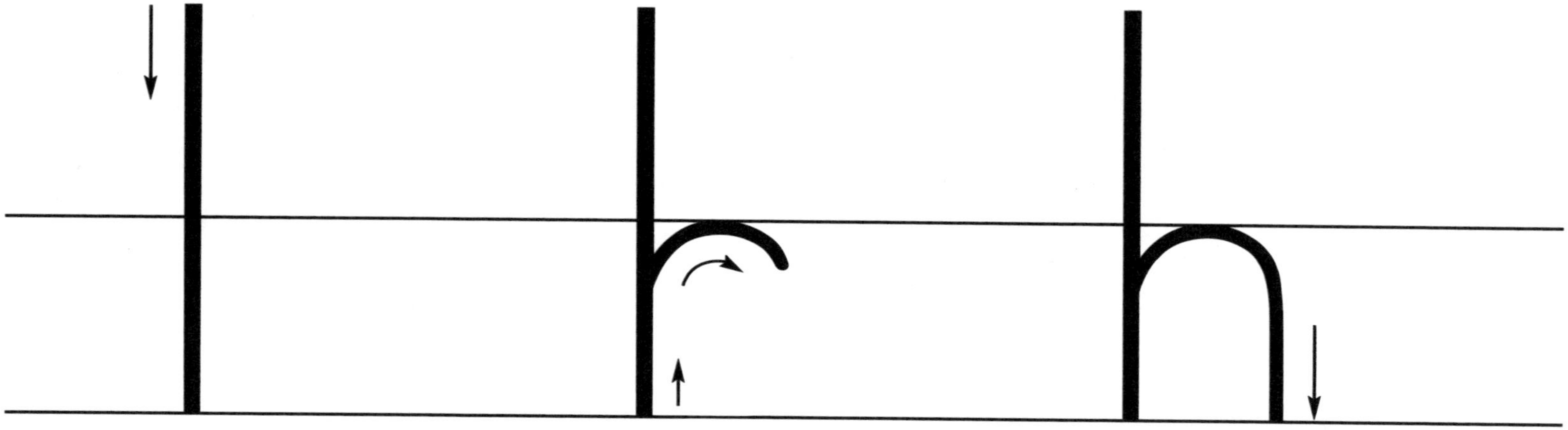

dive down

swim up
and over

down

Start on the dot. Copy h.

☑ Check h

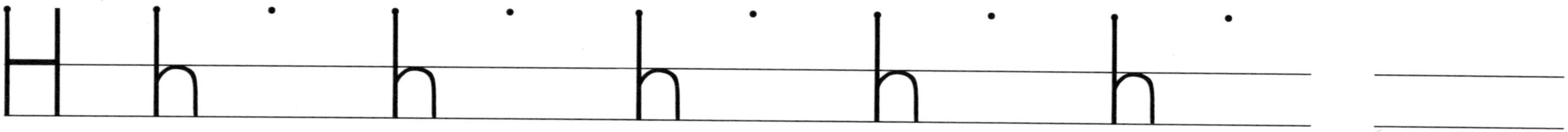

H is for horse.

56 My Printing Book

© 2022 Learning Without Tears

Draw a mane.

Copy capital H.

Copy lowercase h.

Copy the sentences.

Horses are mammals.

They have hairy manes.

☐ Check Sentence

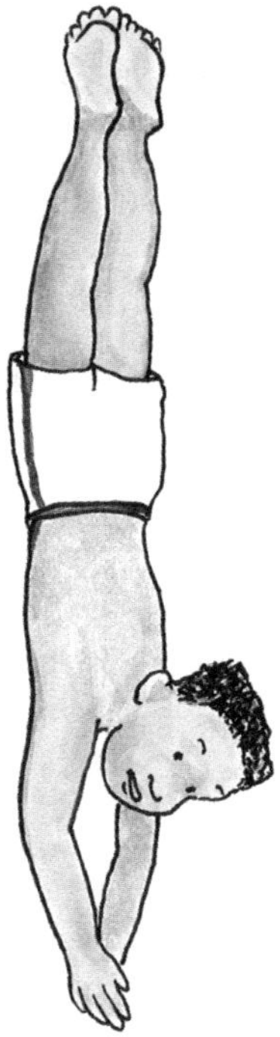

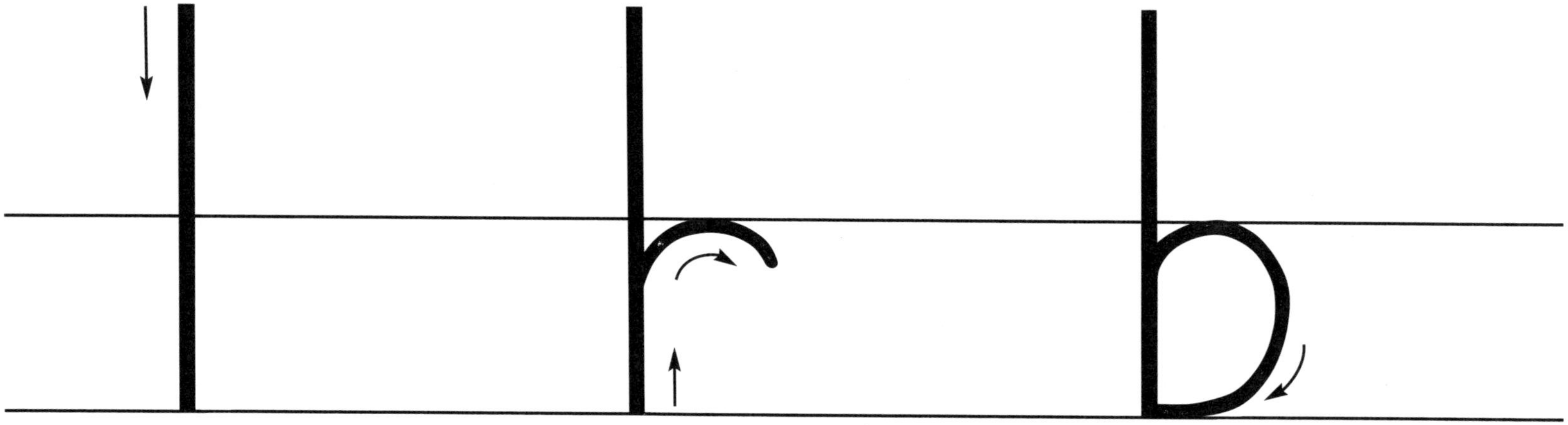

dive down swim up and over around bump

Start on the dot. Copy b. ☐ Check b

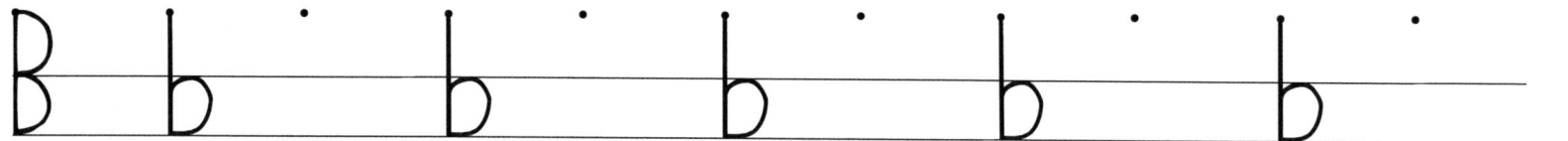

B is for **b**icycle.

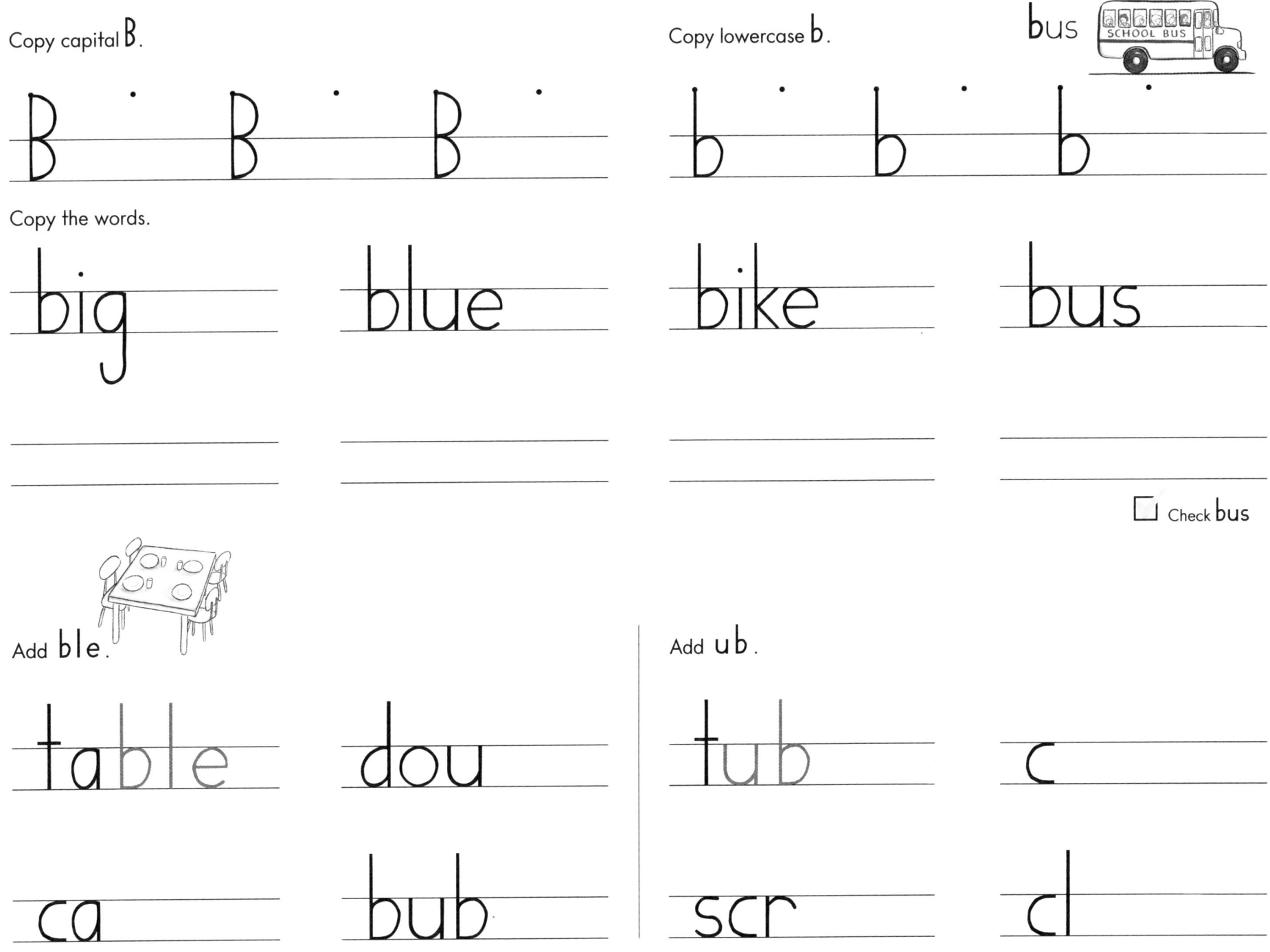

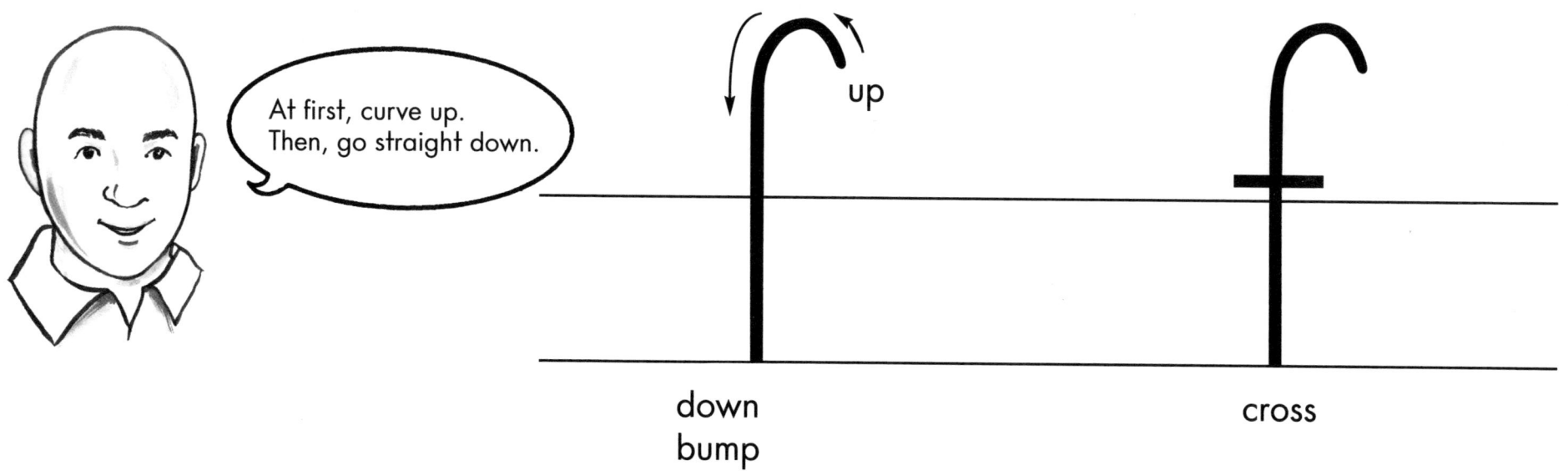

Start on the dot. Copy f. ☑ Check f

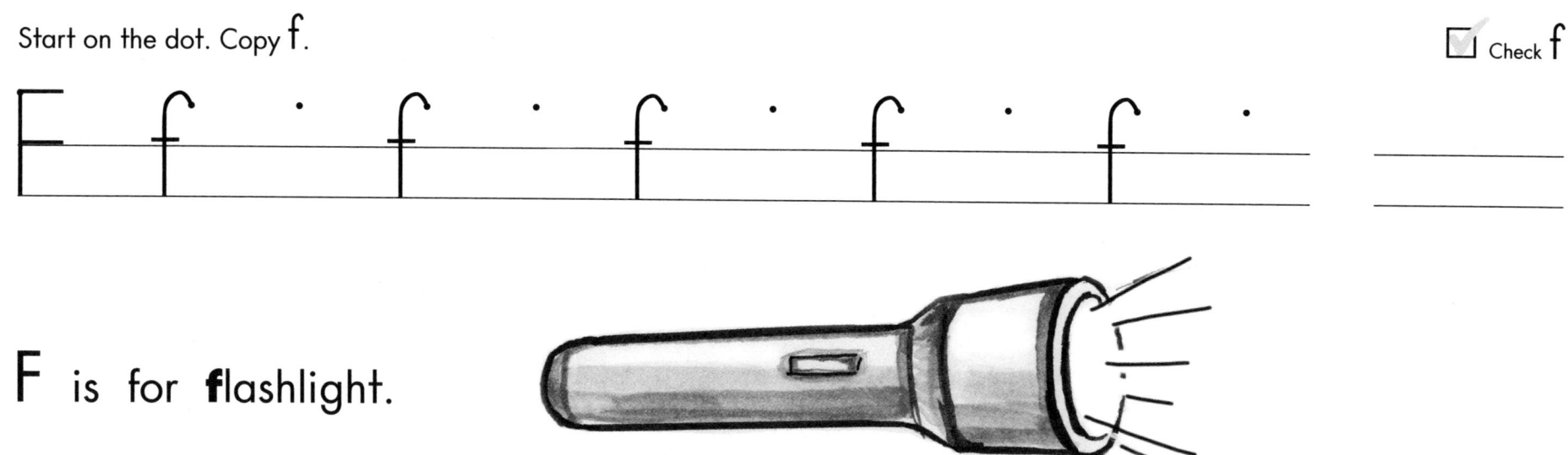

F is for **f**lashlight.

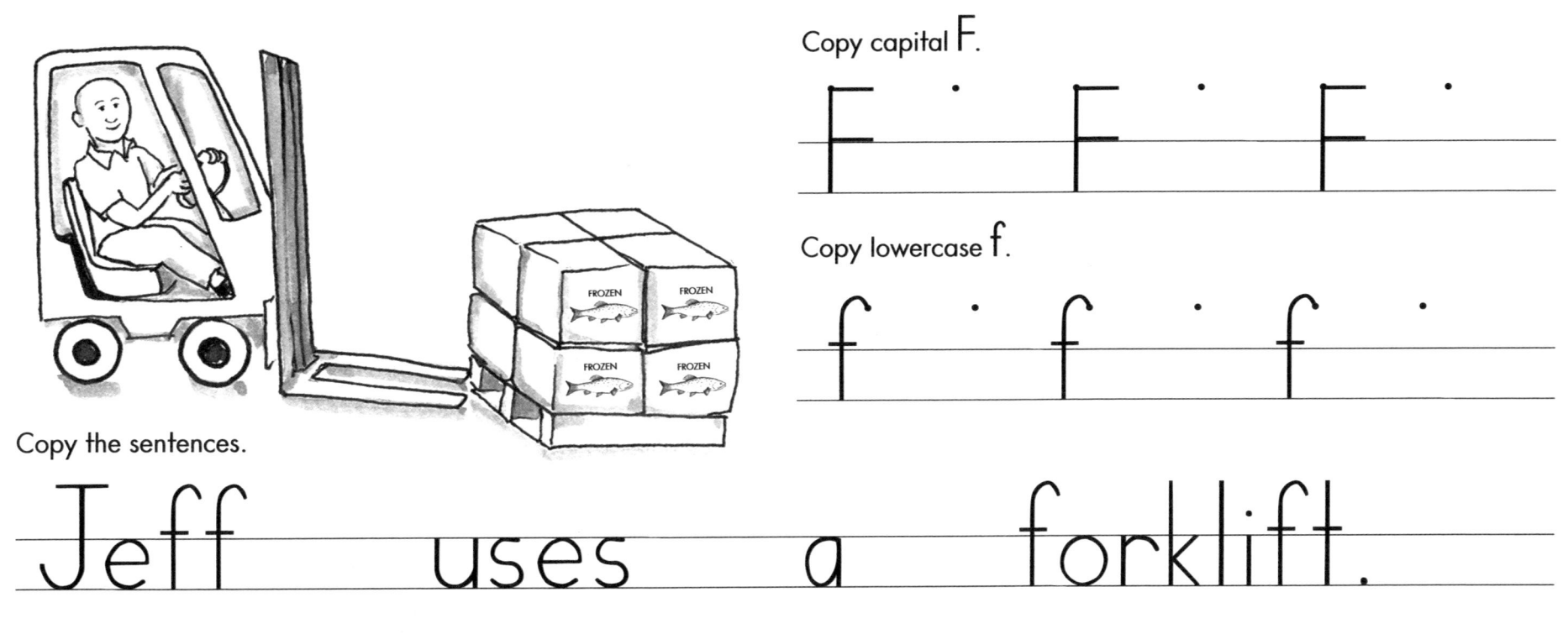

Copy capital F.

Copy lowercase f.

Copy the sentences.

Jeff uses a forklift.

The fork is in front.

☐ Check Sentence

bump

c — Magic c

d — up like a 🚁

q — back down

q — U-turn

Start on the dot. Copy q.   ☑ Check q

Q q · q · q · q · q ·

Q is for quails.

Copy capital Q.

Q   Q   Q

Copy lowercase q.

q   q   q

quilt

Copy the words.

quilt

quilt

quiet

quiet

quit

quit

squid

squid

equal

equal

☐ Check **equal**

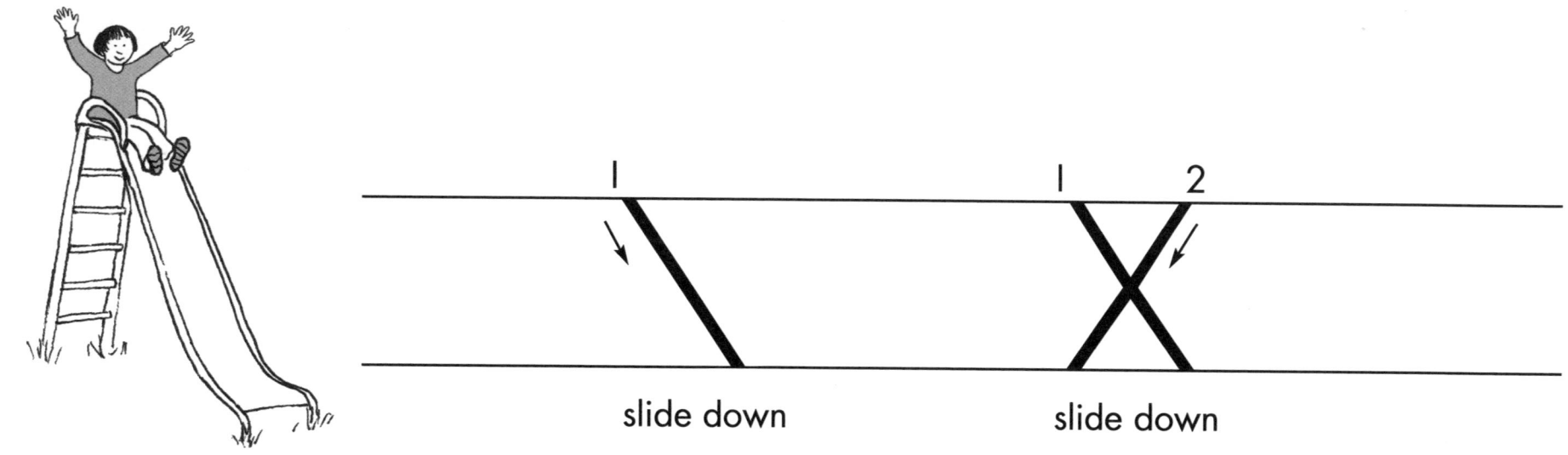

Start on the dot. Copy X. ☑ Check X

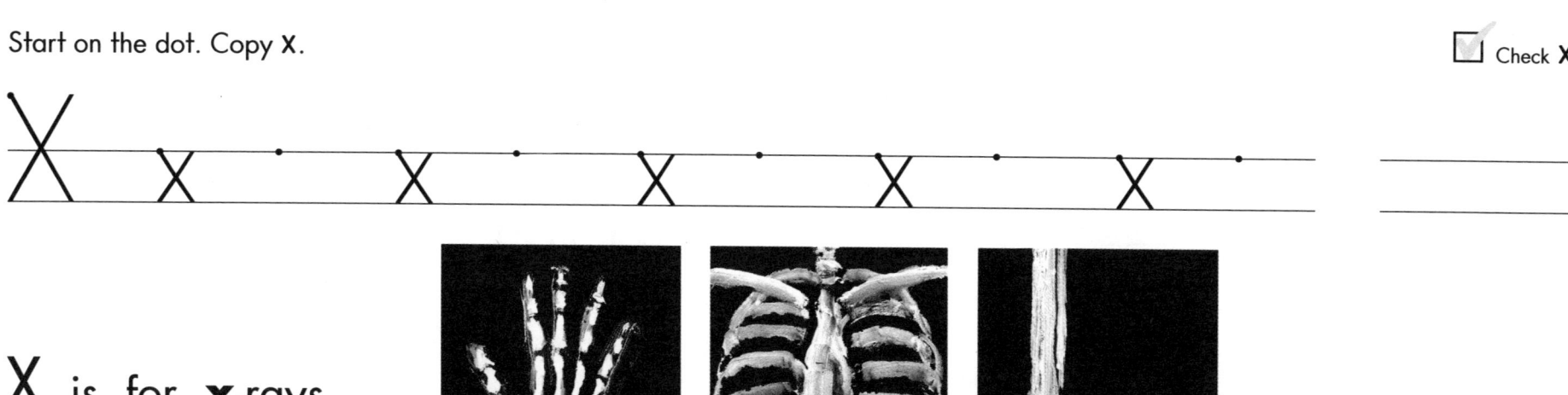

X is for x-rays.

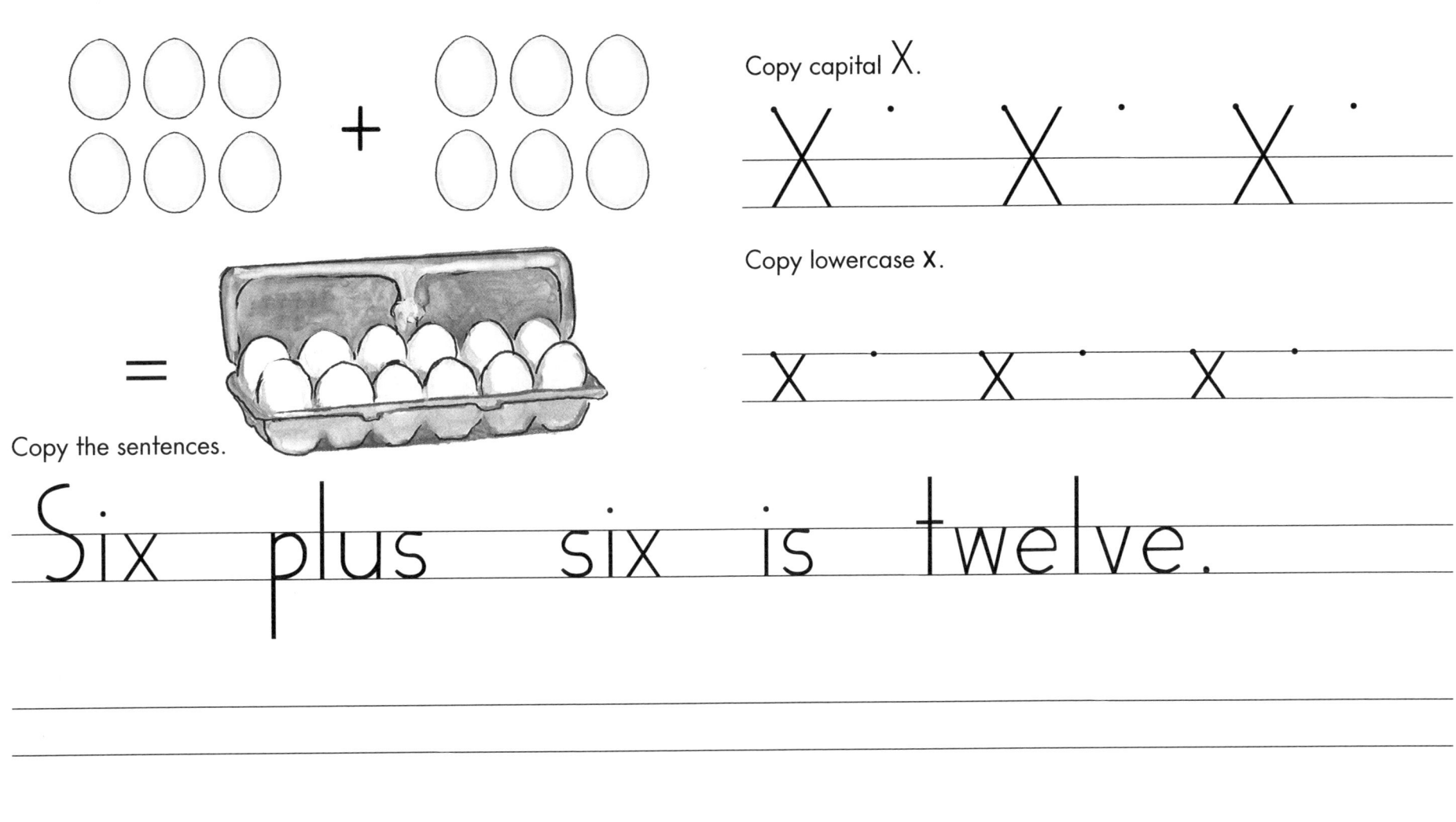

Copy capital X.

Copy lowercase x.

Copy the sentences.

Six plus six is twelve.

Half of twelve is six.

☐ Check Sentence

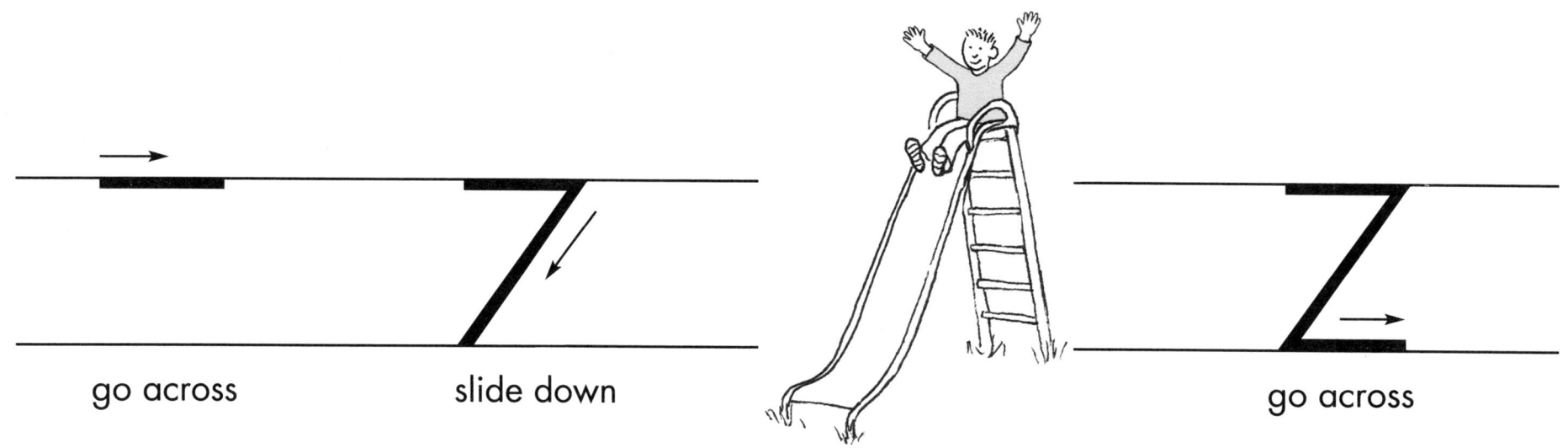

go across   slide down   go across

Start on the dot. Copy Z. ☐ Check Z

Z is for zucchini.

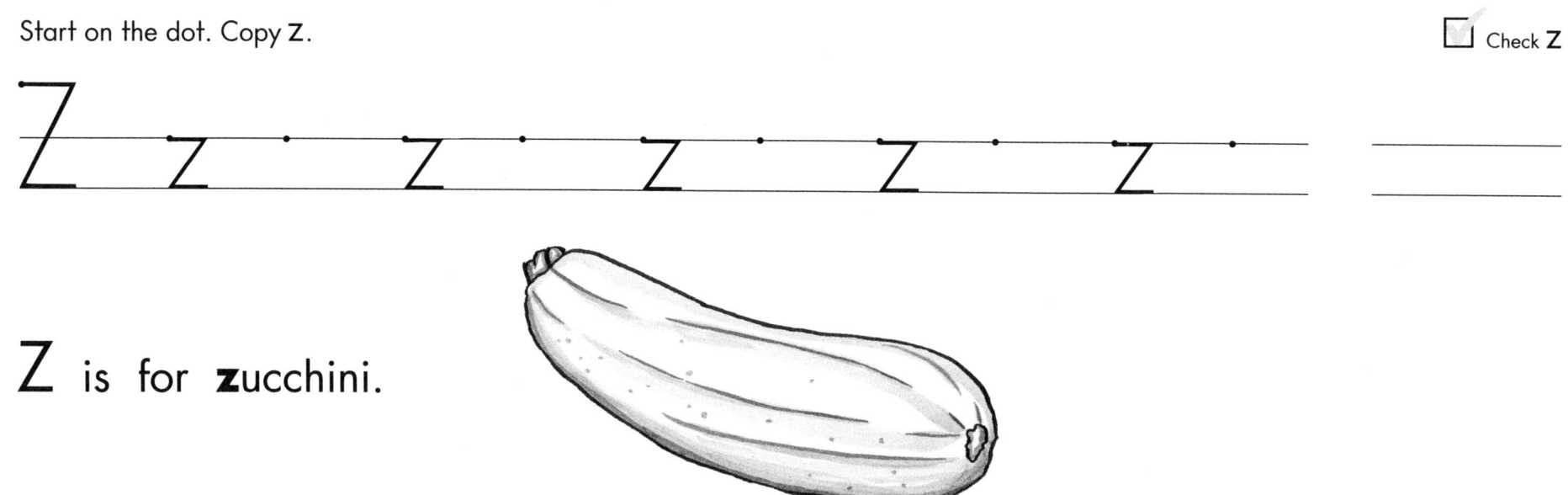

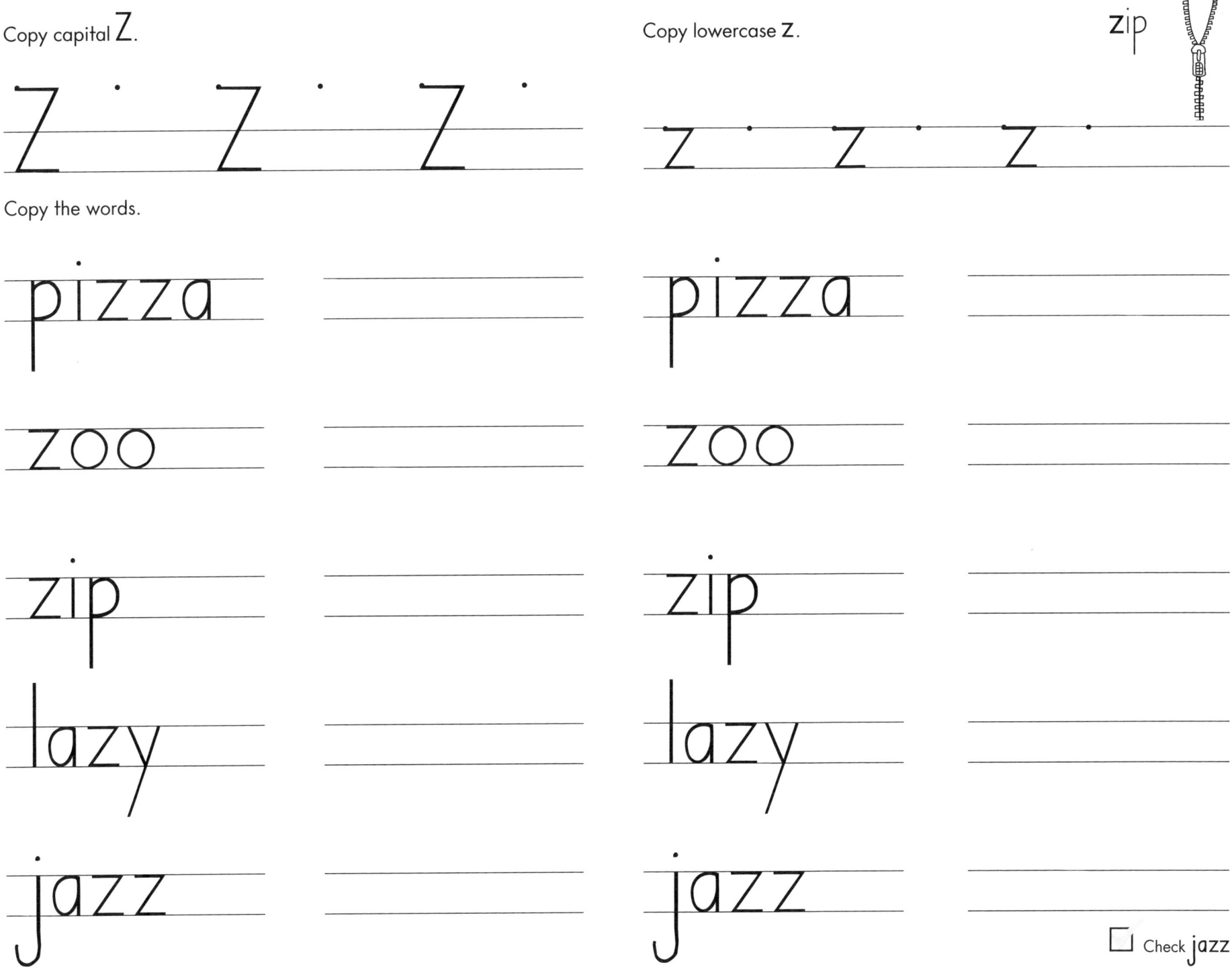

WORDS

Fill in the blanks to make compound words.

tooth + brush =  t____b____

book + case = b___ c___

hot + dog = 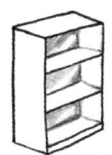 h__d__

foot + ball = f___b___

rain +  bow =  r___b__

lady + bug =  l___b__

POEM

Teeth

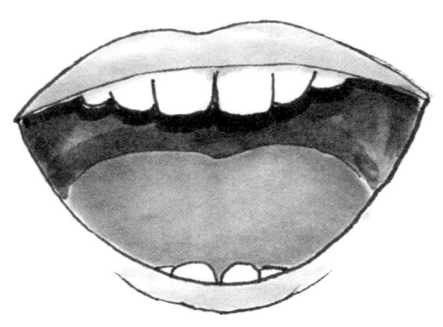

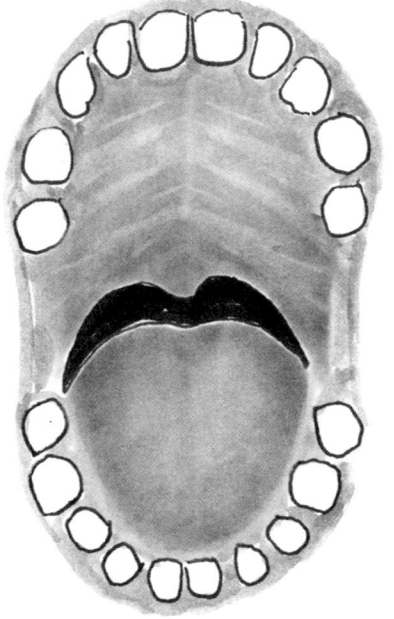

Front teeth bite,

Back teeth chew,

Teeth are shaped

For what they do.

SENTENCES

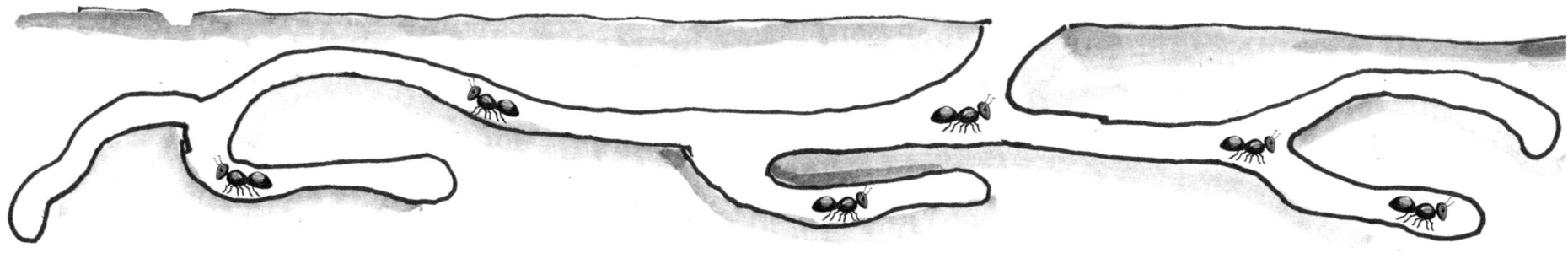

Ants dig little tunnels.

People dig big tunnels.

☐ Check Sentence

PARAGRAPH

Beavers build stick and mud dams. People build concrete dams.

☐ Check Sentence

CHANT

One Potato, Two Potatoes

One 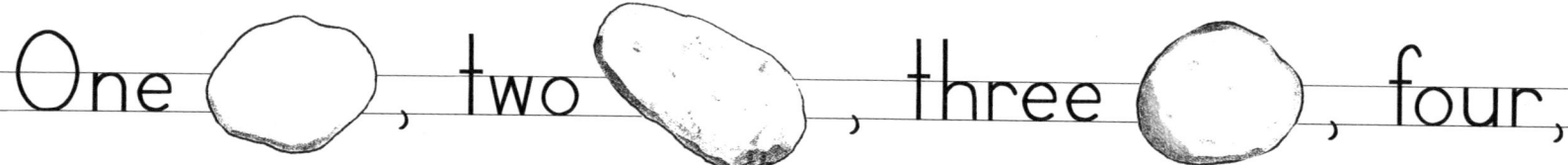, two , three , four,

Five , six , seven , more!

Eight 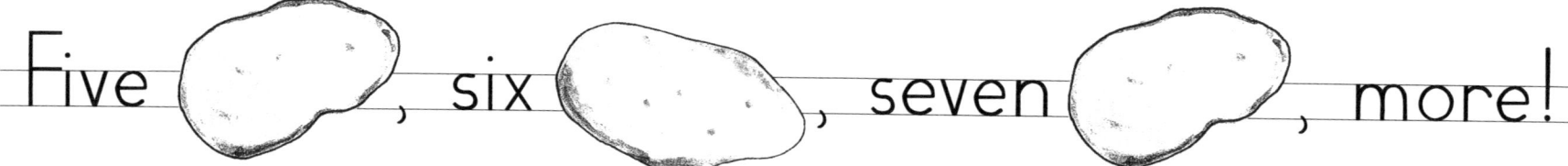, nine , ten , all.

What kind of potatoes do you like?

I like

POEM

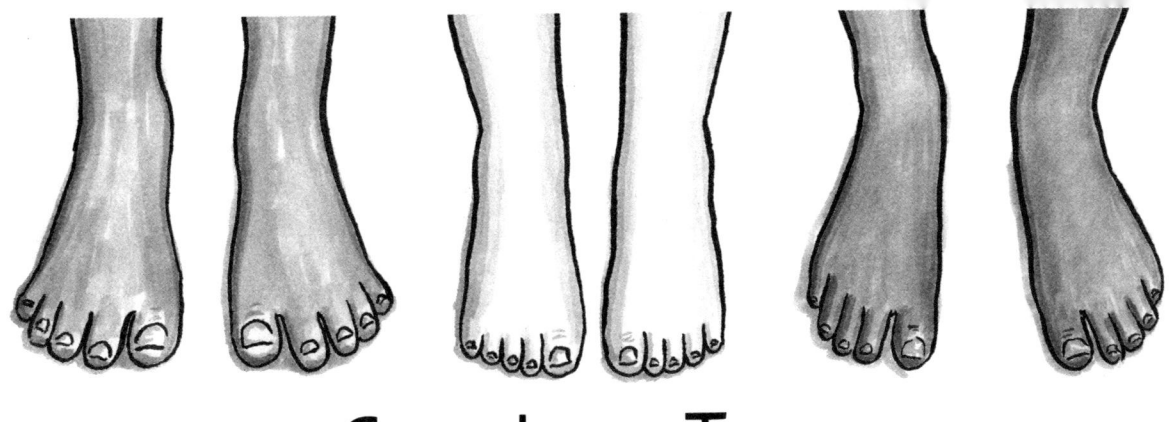

Counting Toes

We are counting toes,

How many do you see?

Ten, twenty, I see thirty!

PARAGRAPH

fish   frog   turtle   bird

Copy.

Many animals have bones.

You can't see their bones.

Listen and write.

The

Teacher dictates: The bones are inside them.

PARAGRAPH

Copy.

Some animals have hard shells.

You can see them. They are outside.

Listen and write.

S

VOWELS

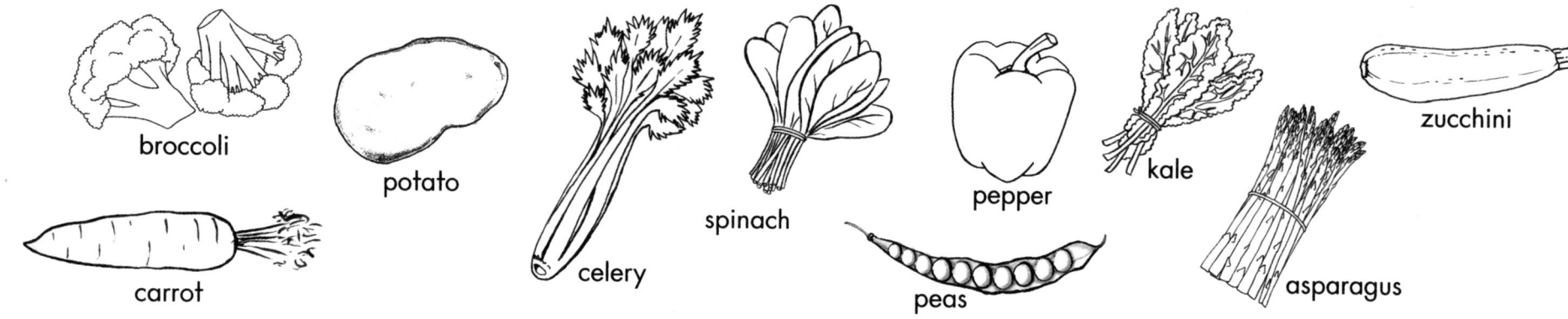

Vegetable Vowels   a e i o u + y

Add the missing vowels.

1. _sp_r_g_s

2. br_cc_l_

3. c_rr_t

4. c_l_r_

5. k_l_

6. p__s

7. p_pp_r

8. p_t_t_

9. sp_n_ch

10. z_cch_n_

POEM

Looking for Carrots

Where can they be?

Under the ground,

Hiding from me!

Where do carrots grow?

Carrots

QUESTION & ANSWER

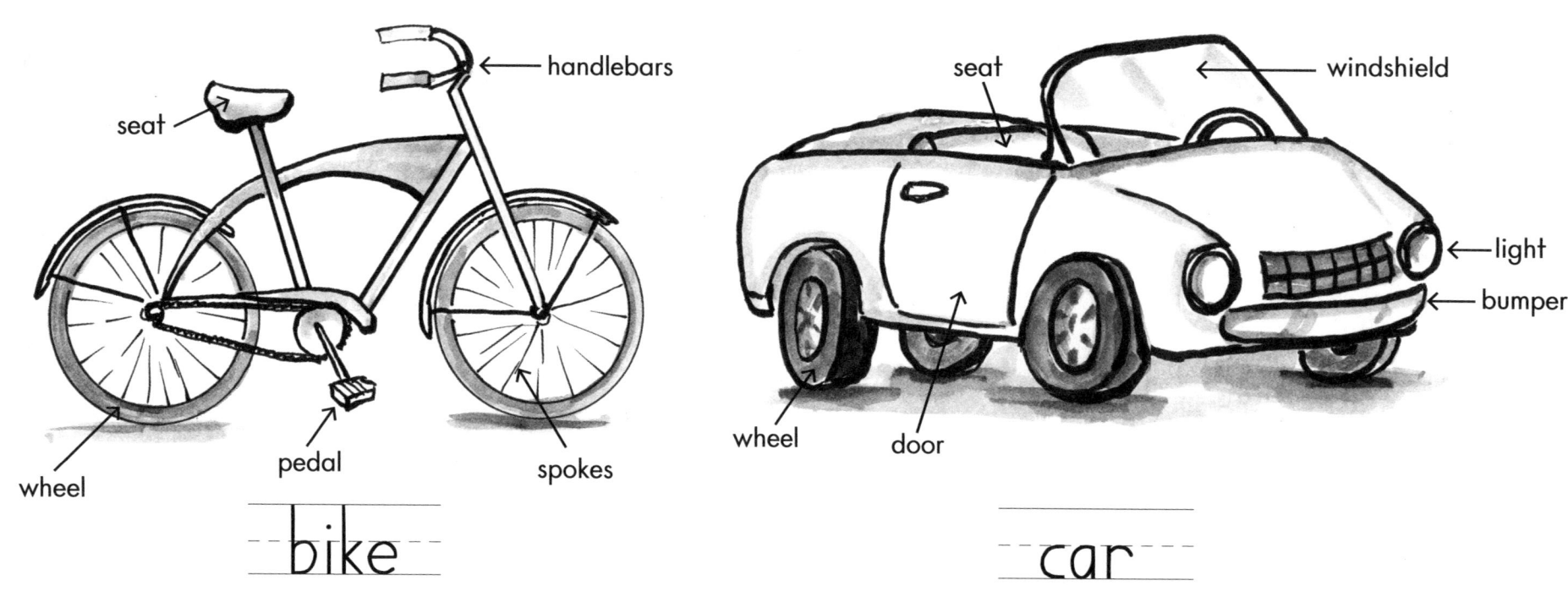

bike

car

Answer the questions with complete sentences.

Which one has handlebars?

The

Which one has a windshield?

The

☐ Check Sentence

PARAGRAPH

Draw the dirt. Then, copy.

1.
2.
3.

First, the truck gets dirt.

Then, it goes to the job site.

Finally, it dumps the dirt.

☐ Check Sentence

ABBREVIATIONS

Months

Jan.   Feb.   Mar.   Apr.

May   June   July   Aug.

Sept.   Oct.   Nov.   Dec.

School Days

Mon.   Tues.   Wed.   Thurs.   Fri.

☑ Check Fri.

CAPITALS

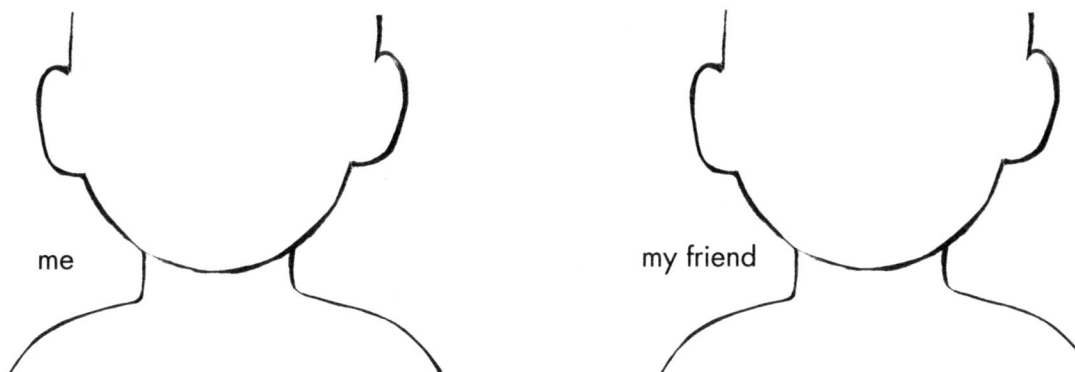

Finish the sentences with correct capitalization.

My initials are ___ ___ ___.

My name is

My friend is

I live in

Today is

My birthday is in

WORDS

| ate | sell | dear | knew | know |
| write | plain | way | toe | won |

Find and write the homophone.

1. eight _____
2. cell _____
3. deer _____
4. new _____
5. no _____

6. right _____
7. plane _____
8. weigh _____
9. tow _____
10. one _____

☐ Check **won**

Choose a homophone pair.
Write two sentences.

_____
_____

WRITING

Complete the words. Then, complete the sentence.

1 cent = penny
5 cents = nickel
10 cents = dime
25 cents = quarter
100 cents = dollar

 one p _____

 one n _____

 one d _____

 one q _____

one d _____

ten d _____

If I had ten dollars, I would _____

SYLLABLES

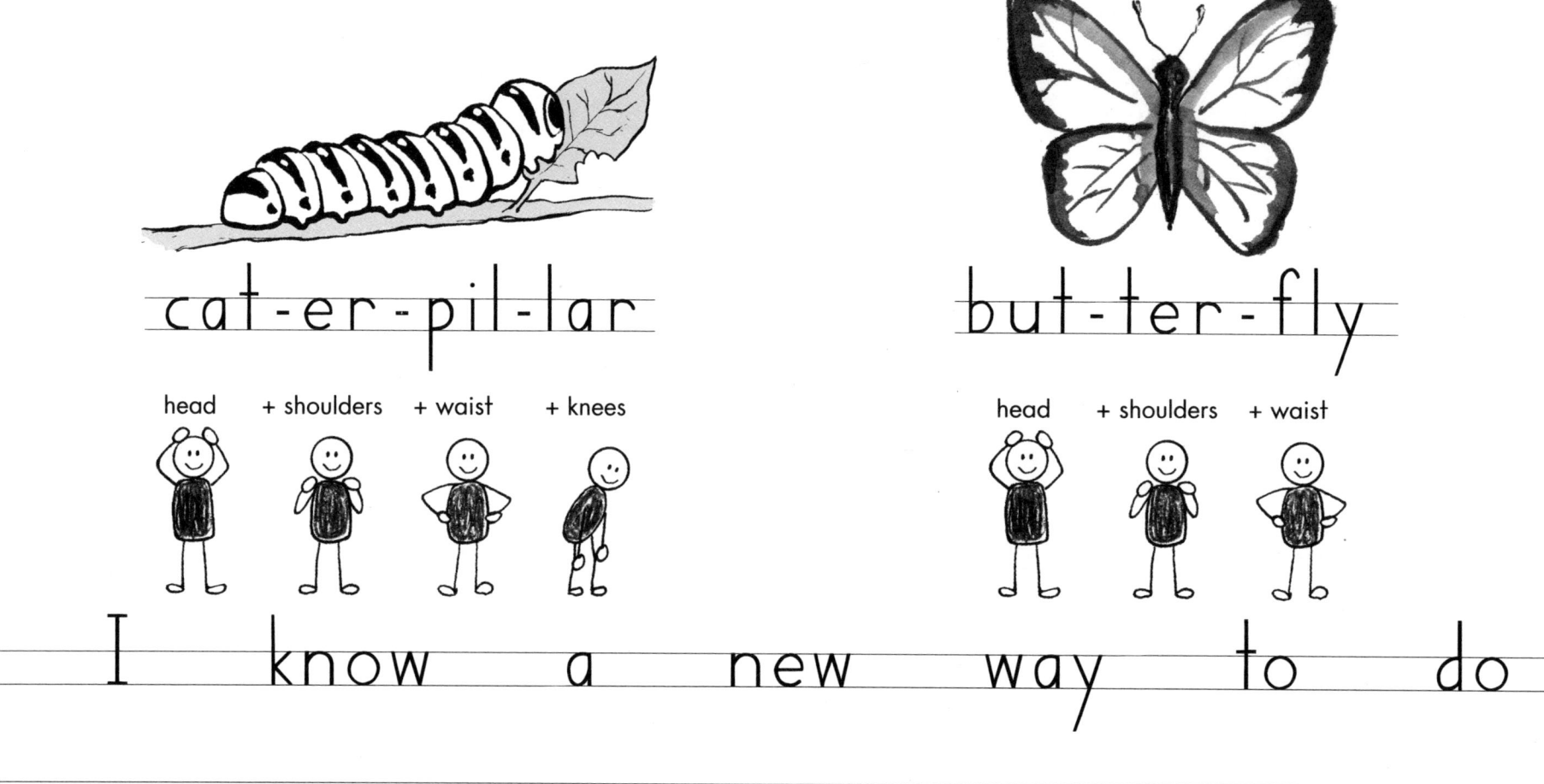

cat-er-pil-lar   but-ter-fly

I know a new way to do

syllables. Watch me move!

☑ Check Sentence

PARAGRAPH

ant   grasshopper

dragonfly

praying mantis

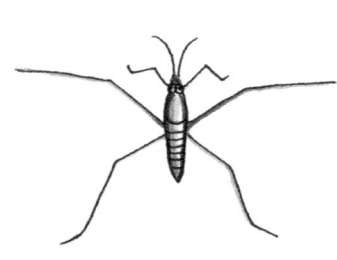

water strider

Copy.

Insects have six legs. Insects walk on walls or fly.

Listen and write.

A few

Teacher dictates: A few walk on water.

SENTENCES

behind the chair
on the table
in the chair
beside the chair
under the table

Look at the picture. Finish each sentence.

The girl is

The table is

The bird is

The ball

The book

☐ Check Sentence

SENTENCES

| ~~pig~~ | dog | turtle | duck | snail |
| ~~first~~ | second | third | fourth | fifth |

Put the animals in order.

The pig was first.

The _____ was _____

The _____ was _____

The _____ was _____

The _____ was _____

Then, what happened?

Numbers on the Slate Chalkboard

Teacher writes 4 with chalk.

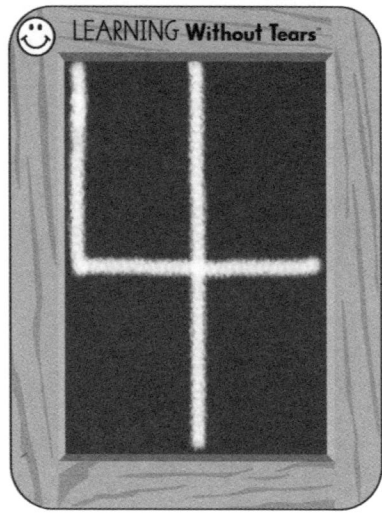

Child wets 4 with a little sponge.

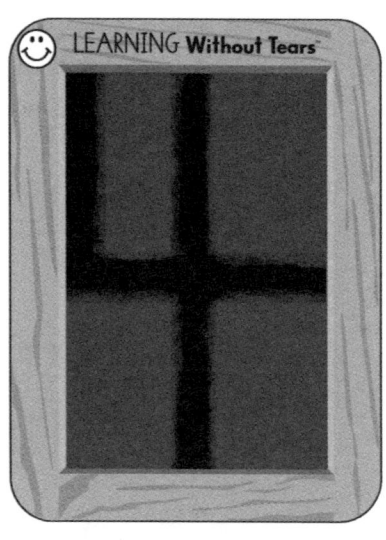

WET

Child dries 4 with a paper towel.

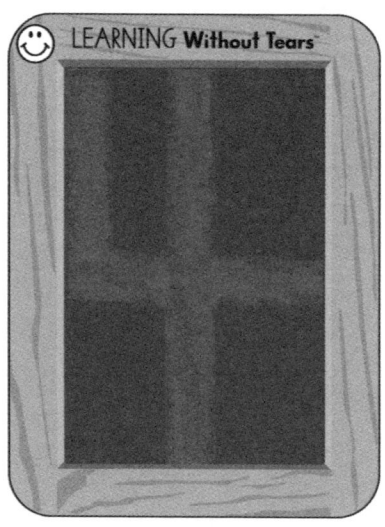

DRY

Child writes 4 with chalk.

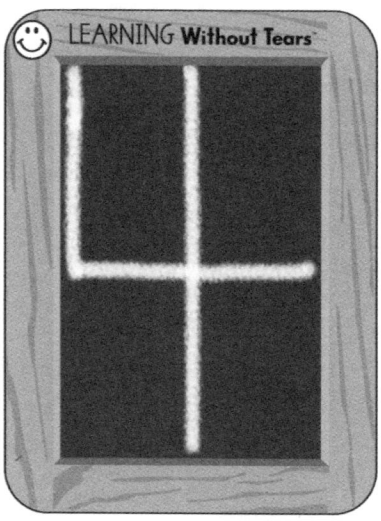

TRY

Numbers on Gray Blocks

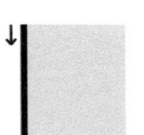  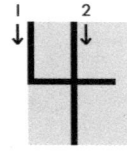  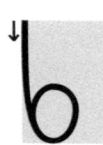 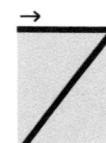 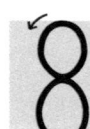 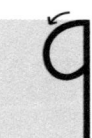

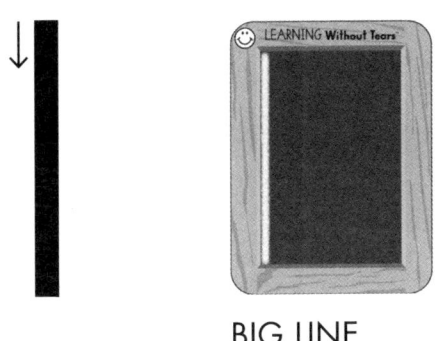

BIG LINE

Copy 1.

| | | | L | L |

☐ Check 1

Copy.

one

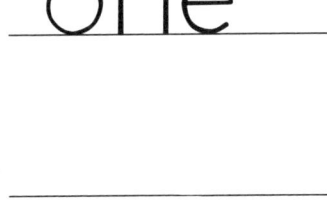

1 goose

BIG CURVE + LITTLE LINE

Copy 2.

2 2 2 2 2

☐ Check 2

Copy.

two

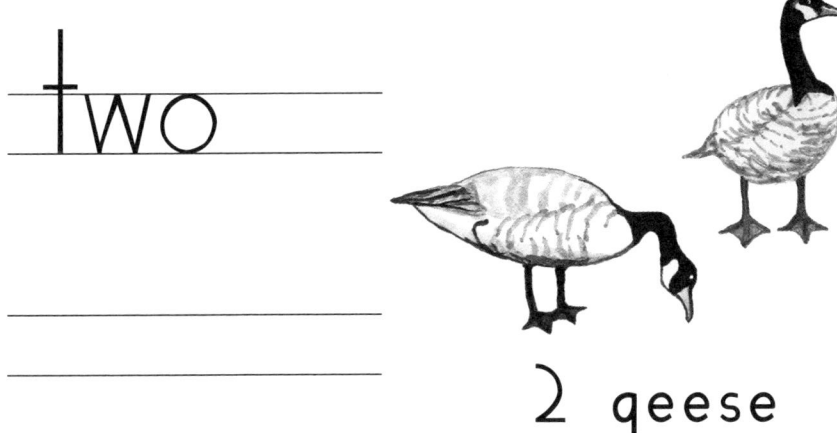

2 geese

My Printing Book

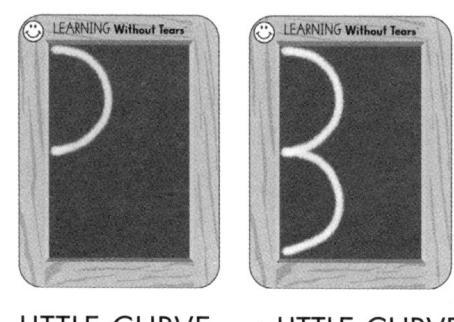

LITTLE CURVE   + LITTLE CURVE

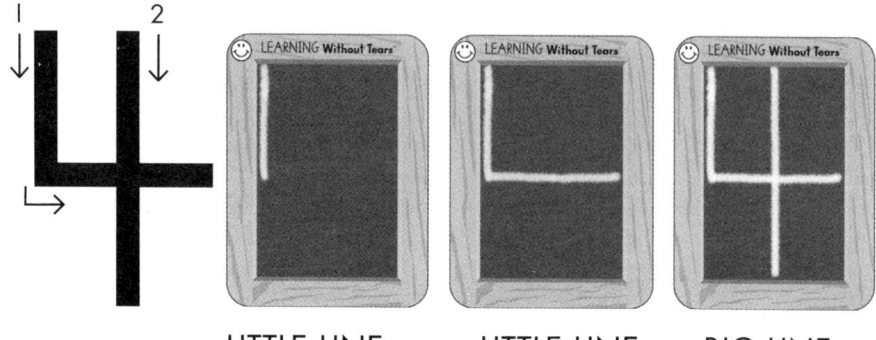

LITTLE LINE   + LITTLE LINE   + BIG LINE

Copy 3.

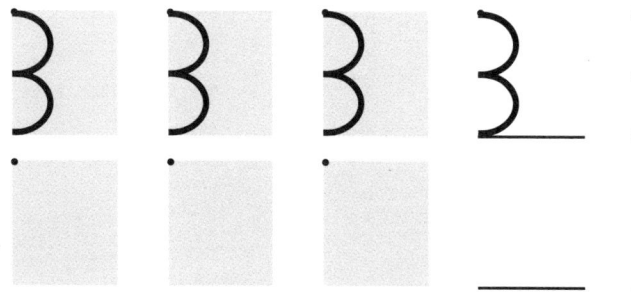

☐ Check 3

Copy.

3 fish

Copy 4.

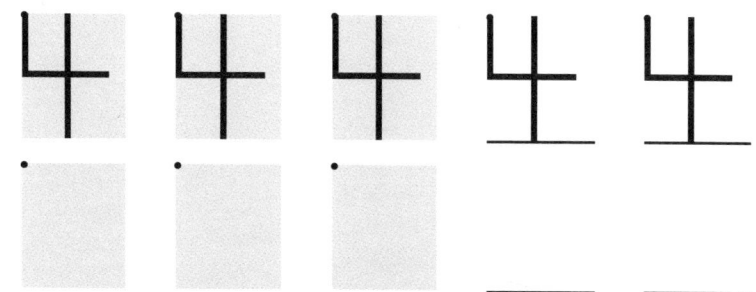

☐ Check 4

Copy.

four

4 snowmen

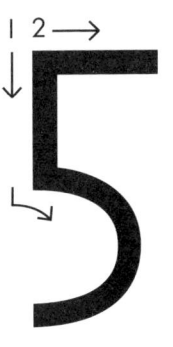
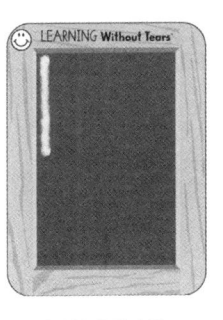 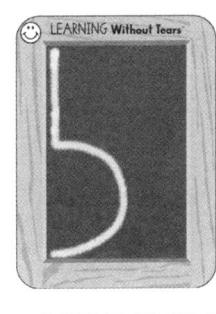 

LITTLE LINE + LITTLE CURVE + LITTLE LINE

Copy .

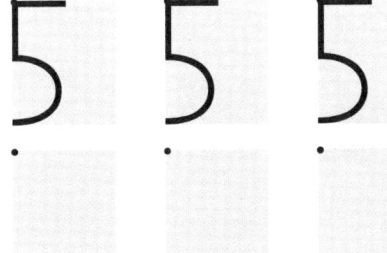

☐ Check 5

Copy.

five

5 umbrellas

  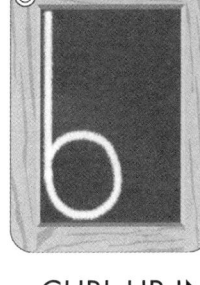

BIG LINE + CURL UP IN THE CORNER

Copy 6.

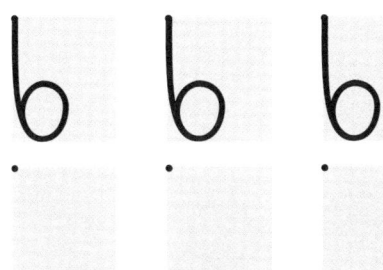

☐ Check 6

Copy.

six

6 bears

My Printing Book 91

7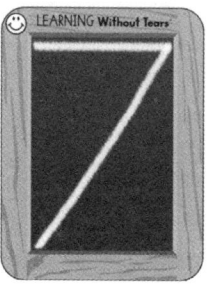

LITTLE LINE + BIG LINE

Copy 7.

☑ Check 7

Copy.

seven

7 plants

8

BEGIN WITH S + UP TO THE TOP

Copy 8.

8 8 8 8 8

☑ Check 8

Copy.

eight

8 spiders

  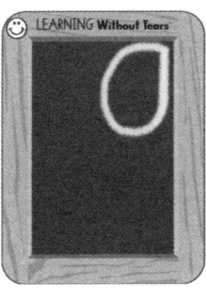 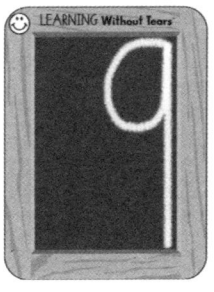

LITTLE CURVE   + UP   + BIG LINE

Copy 9.

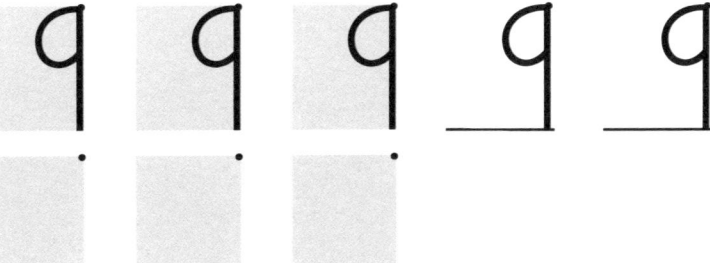

☐ Check 9

Copy.

nine

1 2 3
4 5 6
7 8 9

9 numbers

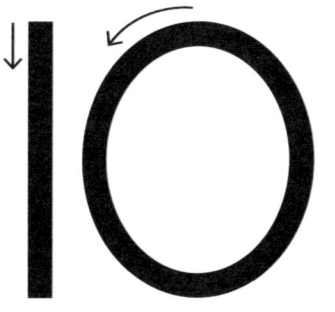  

BIG LINE   BIG CURVE + GO AROUND

Copy 10.

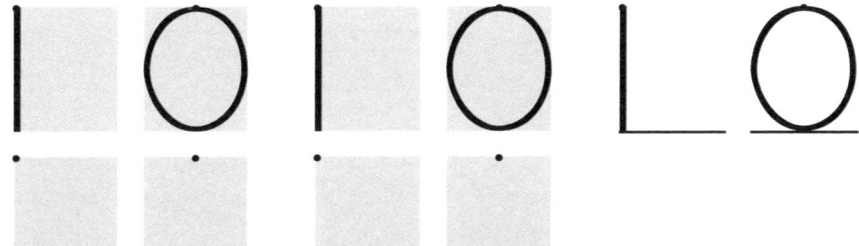

☐ Check 10

Copy.

ten

10 balloons

FINAL CHECK

Name_____   Date_____

☑ Write and check the capital alphabet.

A ___ ___ ___ ___ ___ ___ ___ ___ ___

___ ___ ___ ___ ___ ___ ___ ___ ___

___ ___ ___ ___ ___ ___ ___ ___

☑ Write and check the lowercase alphabet.

a ___ ___ ___ ___ ___ ___ ___ ___ ___

___ ___ ___ ___ ___ ___ ___ ___ ___

___ ___ ___ ___ ___ ___ ___ ___

☑ Write and check numbers one to ten.

1 ___ ___ ___ ___ ___ ___ ___ ___ ___